Volume **8** **THE**
GOLDEN BOOK ENCYCLOPEDIA

Gabon to heredity

ga-he

An exciting, up-to-date encyclopedia
in 20 fact-filled, entertaining volumes

Especially designed as
a first encyclopedia for
today's grade-school children

More than 2,500 full-color
photographs and illustrations

GOLDEN ®

From the Publishers of Golden® Books

Western Publishing Company, Inc.
Racine, Wisconsin 53404

©MCMLXXXVIII
Western Publishing Company, Inc.

GOLDEN®, GOLDEN BOOK®, GOLDEN & DESIGN® and the GOLDEN BOOK ENCYCLOPEDIA
are trademarks of Western Publishing Company, Inc. No part of this book may be reproduced
or copied in any form without written permission from the publisher.
Printed in the United States of America.

ILLUSTRATION CREDITS
(t=top, b=bottom, c=center, l=left, r=right)

COVER CREDITS

Library of Congress Catalog Card Number: 87-82741
ISBN: 0-307-70108-5

ABCDEFGHIJKLM

The letter *G* started as a symbol for a boomerang. It came from the Egyptians' picture writing.

The Greeks called this letter *gamma*, wrote it as a right angle, and gave it a hard *g* sound.

The Romans used a symbol for the hard *g* sound that looked like our capital *G*.

Gabon, *see* Africa

galaxy

Astronomers describe a galaxy as a giant cluster of stars. A galaxy may contain billions or even trillions of stars. Its diameter may range from a few thousand to a half-billion light-years. A *light-year* is the distance that light travels in a year—about 9½ trillion kilometers (5 trillion miles). Galaxies are held together by the force of gravity. (*See* **gravity.**)

Our sun and the planets of our solar system are on the edge of a galaxy called the Milky Way. The Andromeda galaxy, which can be seen from Earth, is much larger than the Milky Way. It is 125,000 light-years across and contains an estimated 400 billion stars. (*See* **Milky Way** and **solar system.**)

Most galaxies are spiral or elliptical in shape. A *spiral galaxy* looks like a pinwheel. Some of its stars form a thick clump at the center. Its other stars form curved arms stretching out from it. The Milky Way and Andromeda galaxies are both spiral galaxies. An *elliptical galaxy* is egg-shaped. There are also *irregular galaxies.*

Galileo

Galileo Galilei was an Italian mathematician and astronomer who lived from 1564 to 1642. He was interested in how things move. He had new ideas about the relationship between gravity and *mass*—density. Galileo showed that two objects always fall at the same speed, even if one is heavier than the other. According to one story, Galileo did this by dropping two objects of unequal weight from the Leaning Tower of Pisa in Italy.

A spiral galaxy as seen from the side in a telescopic photograph.

The telescope is one of Galileo's many important discoveries.

In 1609, Galileo heard of the telescope, a new Dutch invention. He set out to reinvent the telescope for himself. He was able to make more powerful telescopes than the Dutch had. Galileo used his telescopes to observe the planets and stars. With them, he discovered that the moon's surface is pockmarked by craters and that the sun has sunspots and rotates. He also discovered the four largest moons of Jupiter and saw the phases of Venus. What he saw convinced him that the earth revolves around the sun. He decided that all objects—on earth and in the heavens—obey the same laws of motion.

Galileo made important discoveries, but the method he used to develop his ideas was even more important. He carefully observed how objects and planets move. Then he used experiments and mathematics to confirm his observations. Modern scientists still work in this way.

See also **astronomy** and **experiment.**

Gama, Vasco da, *see* da Gama, Vasco

Gambia, *see* Africa

Gandhi, Mahatma

Mohandas K. Gandhi (GHAN-dee) was a great leader who helped India become an independent country. Gandhi used peaceful ways to win his goals. He was so admired that he was given the title Mahatma, meaning "Great Soul."

Gandhi was born in India in 1869, and studied law in India and England. In 1893, he went to South Africa. At that time, South Africa, like India, was under British control. Gandhi saw that dark-skinned people living there, including Indians, were being treated unfairly. He decided to give up his law practice and become a political leader. He gave up Western customs, such as wearing suits. For the rest of his life, he wore a loincloth and shawl, like the peasants of India. He tried to live by the ideals of the Hindu religion. (*See* **Hinduism.**)

In 1915, after winning new laws that helped the Indians in South Africa, Gandhi returned to India. There he became a leader in the movement for a free India. The struggle against the British lasted more than 30 years. During this time, Gandhi also worked to help India's millions of poor.

Gandhi's chief weapon was what he called *satyagraha*—"soul force." This was a way of protesting government laws and actions in a peaceful way. To use "soul force," a person must be brave and believe in truth. In 1930, Gandhi used *satyagraha* to protest a British law that Indians must buy salt only from the government. Gandhi led hundreds of people on a march to the sea, where they made salt from seawater. Even though some of his followers were attacked, they did not fight back. The British later changed the salt law. This march, and similar actions, made a great impression on the entire world.

Gandhi was influenced also by Islamic and Christian teachings. All his life, he tried to persuade people to return love for hate. Although he was often attacked and imprisoned, he refused to give up or speak angrily of those who harmed him.

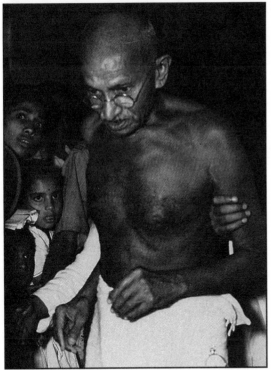

Mohandas Gandhi was a teacher who helped India gain independence in the 1940s.

India gained its independence in 1947. But it was soon split into two countries—India for Hindus, and Pakistan for Muslims. Gandhi was unhappy about this division. In 1948, Gandhi was shot and killed by a Hindu man who disagreed with his way of thinking. Gandhi's ideas, however, later influenced other great leaders, such as Martin Luther King, Jr.

Ganges River

The Ganges (GAHN-geez) is the longest river in India and one of the largest in the world. Followers of the Hindu religion in India believe the Ganges is a sacred river. They call it *Ganga Mai,* "Mother Ganges." Allahabad, Hardwar, and Benares are holy cities along the Ganges. Here and in other places Hindus bathe in the river. They believe that the water cures illness and washes away sin.

The Ganges begins high in the Himalayas. It flows southeast through northern India and across the country of Bangladesh. It joins the Brahmaputra River as it empties into the Bay of Bengal. Here, the two rivers form a large, low plain called a *delta.*

More than 200 million people live in the Ganges valley. Calcutta is the largest city in the valley. New Delhi, India's capital, is on the Jumna River. The Jumna River is a *tributary* of the Ganges River. This means that it flows into the Ganges. Dozens of tributaries flow into the Ganges during its nearly 1,600-mile (2,500-kilometer) course. The waters of the Ganges are used to irrigate farmland. The lower part of the river is used to send goods to different cities.

Garfield, James, *see* presidents of the U.S.

gas

There are three familiar phases of matter—solid, liquid, and gas. Water, for example, can be a liquid, or frozen into a solid (ice), or heated until it turns into a gas (water vapor). At each phase, matter is still made of molecules, but the molecules move differently. It is the way they move that gives each phase its properties.

In solids, the molecules move only slightly. So the solid keeps a definite shape. Molecules in a liquid can slip past each other. Molecules in a gas fly off in all directions, often bouncing off each other. Liquids and gases take on the shape of their containers. You can pour liquids, but you can't pour gases, because the gas molecules spread so far apart. For this reason, gases are usually much lighter than liquids or solids.

Heat affects the movement of molecules. If solids are heated enough, they melt into a liquid. If liquids are heated enough, they boil into a gas. The more heat, the faster the molecules move and the farther apart they get.

Some materials are gases even at room temperature. Air contains some of the most common gases—nitrogen, oxygen, water vapor, and carbon dioxide.

Natural gas, a mixture of gases, is often used for fuel. (*See* **gas, natural.**)

See also **evaporation; heat;** and **matter.**

gas, natural

Thousands of years ago, people in China discovered that a colorless gas was escaping from the earth through cracks in the ground. They found that the gas would burn. They learned to use hollow bamboo poles as pipes for the gas. Then they could use the gas for cooking and heating. This is the gas we call natural gas.

Since both natural gas and gasoline are often called "gas," it is easy to confuse them. Both contain carbon and hydrogen. But gasoline is a liquid, not a gas.

Today, natural gas is one of the world's most important fuels. It provides about one fourth of the total fuel energy used in the United States. Many people use natural gas for cooking and heating. The chemical industry uses it to make many products, such as detergents, drugs, and plastics.

In the late 1800s, people in the United States learned to capture natural gas from underground wells and send it long distances through pipes. At first, gas was used mostly for lighting. (There were no electric lights yet.)

In the early 1900s, huge amounts of natural gas were found in Texas, Louisiana, and Oklahoma. The natural gas was discovered as people drilled into the earth in search of oil. At first, natural gas was not recognized as a valuable fuel. It was often allowed to escape or was burned near the oil well. (*See* **oil** and **oil drilling.**)

By the 1930s, people had found ways to store large amounts of gas and transport it in pipelines. Long stretches of pipe allowed gas to be sent from the Southwest to other parts of the United States. After that, natural gas was widely used as a fuel.

Scientists believe that natural gas began to form millions of years ago. Over the ages, layer after layer of tiny marine animals, plants, and sand settled on the ocean floor. Under the great weight, the chemical compounds changed into natural gas and oil. That is why oil and natural gas are often found together.

Today, the United States still produces more natural gas than any other country. The Soviet Union and the Netherlands are the other major producers.

See also **fuel.**

A workman adjusts flow in a pipeline that carries natural gas across the country. The gas will travel uphill through this curve if pushed along by pressure.

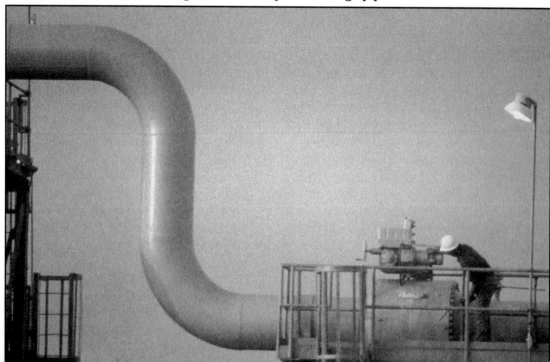

Natural gas is a gas that burns.
It is used as fuel in stoves and furnaces.
Gasoline is a liquid fuel for engines.

gasoline

Gasoline is a fuel made from petroleum oil. To make gasoline, crude oil is *refined*—separated into its chemical parts and treated to make it burn better. In fact, about half of the petroleum used in the United States is in the form of gasoline. Gasoline is used to power the engines of automobiles. Some airplanes, and many small machines, such as lawn mowers and power saws use gasoline, too. (*See* oil.)

Gasoline is called "gas" for short, making it easy to confuse with natural gas. Both are fuels, and both are *hydrocarbons*—substances made up of the chemical elements hydrogen and carbon. But gasoline is a liquid, not a gas.

The treated gasoline used to run an automobile engine has many ingredients besides gasoline. Some are added to keep the engine clean. Some keep the gasoline pure and help the engine run smoothly. Others keep the tanks in cars and gasoline stations from rusting.

See also **automobile; engine;** and **fuel.**

gem

Since ancient times, people have valued certain minerals, stones, and other rocklike substances for their beauty, rarity, or hardness. We call these materials gems. Gems are used for jewelry and in industry.

Some gems, such as diamond, come from crystals. Diamond is the hardest and the rarest gem. When properly cut and polished, a diamond gives off brilliant flashes of light. Diamonds not good enough for jewelry are used for cutting and grinding very hard materials. Diamonds are hard enough to cut glass. They are also long-lasting. Most record players have a diamond needle.

Other gems come from minerals. Emerald is a deep-green variety of a common mineral called beryl. Ruby and sapphire are varieties of the mineral corundum. Ruby is red and sapphire is blue because of elements mixed in with the corundum. For example, iron and titanium make sapphire blue. The first laser used a ruby for its light source.

Pearls and amber are called gems, though they do not come from crystals or minerals. Pearls are produced by oysters. Amber is the golden-yellow fossilized sap of trees.

The opal is another gem known for its beauty. When you turn an opal, brilliant colors appear, disappear, and move around. Some opals form as part of petrified wood. Others are found in volcanic deposits.

See also **crystal; diamond; mineral; pearl;** and **petrified wood.**

An emerald (top) is a green gem in the form of a crystal. A large, deep-red ruby (bottom) is one of the most valuable of all gems.

mechanical energy
generator
electrical energy

N

S

Above, huge generators produce electricity for homes, factories, and offices. Left, a generator changes energy of motion into electricity.

generator

A generator is a machine that produces an electric current. Large electric generators are used in electric power plants. These generators produce electric power that is used in your home. (*See* **electric power.**)

The history of the electric generator dates back to 1819. At that time, there was a great interest in electricity. But electric currents could not be kept flowing for long periods of time. In 1819, a scientist named Hans Christian Oersted accidentally discovered that an electric current causes a compass needle to move. A compass needle is a magnet. (*See* **magnetism.**)

Two other scientists reasoned that if an electric current caused a magnet to move, it was possible that a moving magnet could cause an electric current. These scientists were Michael Faraday of England and Joseph Henry of the United States. In 1830, they each produced short bursts of electricity by moving a magnet near a coil of copper wire. The next year, Faraday used this idea to build the first generator.

In a simple electric generator, a magnet and copper wire are the most important parts. The magnet is usually shaped like a U. The copper wire is coiled inside it and connected to a *rotor*—a drive shaft. As the rotor turns, the wire turns between the poles of the magnet. When the two ends of the coiled wire are connected together, the magnetic field causes electrons in the copper coil to move in the same direction. That flow of electrons is an electric current.

An electric generator in a power plant may be as big as a house. It can provide enough electricity for as many as a million homes. Some electric generators are small enough to hold in your hand. They provide electricity for small electrical devices.

Many homes, factories, and hospitals have emergency generators. They provide electricity when the electricity from an electric power plant is temporarily cut off.

In an electric power plant, the generator is usually powered by steam. Many emergency generators are powered by gasoline or diesel engines.

See also **electricity** and **Faraday, Michael.**

genetics

When a baby bird hatches from an egg, it will grow up to look like its mother and father. A chicken never hatches from a robin's egg. The baby bird will be of the same kind as its parents. In the same way, other living things produce more of their own kind. Maple trees produce maple trees, dogs produce dogs, humans produce humans.

Still, there are many differences among children of the same parents. If a mother cat gives birth to four kittens at the same time, one may be black, one white, and two black-and-white. One of the kittens may grow to be larger than the others. One may be shy, and another may be friendly.

Why do living things produce other living things of the same kind? Why are there differences among children of the same parents? The science of *genetics* looks for answers to these kinds of questions.

Thousands of years ago, people learned that they could breed animals with particular qualities. For example, if only the largest, healthiest cattle were allowed to become parents, their children would usually be large and healthy. In the same way, people bred dogs to do certain jobs and bred chickens and turkeys for good eating. (*See* **animal breeding**.)

Then, about 150 years ago, an Austrian monk named Gregor Mendel became curious about how *traits*—qualities—are passed on from parents to offspring. To try to find the answer, he set up a group of experiments with pea plants.

Mendel found that traits such as flower color did seem to be *inherited*—passed on from parents to offspring. He kept careful records on hundreds of plants and their offspring. The records gave him an idea. Perhaps in a seed there was "something" from the parents that passed a particular trait on. He thought that there might be a different "something" for each trait.

Since then, scientists have shown that many of Mendel's ideas were right. We call the "something" that passes on a trait a *gene*. The study of genes and how living things pass on traits is called genetics. Mendel was the first person to study inheritance scientifically, so he is sometimes called the "father of genetics." (*See* **Mendel, Gregor.**)

What Genes Are In most living things, genes come in pairs. One gene in a pair

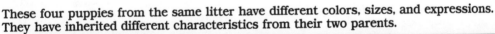

These four puppies from the same litter have different colors, sizes, and expressions. They have inherited different characteristics from their two parents.

comes from one parent, and the other comes from the other parent.

Mendel's experiments with pea plants show how one pair of genes can control one trait. A pea plant has a pair of genes that control what shape seeds it will make. Some pea plants make round seeds, and some have wrinkled seeds.

If both genes in the "seed-shape" pair give directions for round seeds, the plant will make round seeds. If a plant has two genes for wrinkled shape, its seeds are wrinkled.

What if a plant has one gene for round seeds and one for wrinkled seeds? Mendel discovered that these plants produce round seeds. The instructions of the round shape gene covered up the instructions for wrinkled shape. Mendel called the gene for round seeds the *dominant* gene. The gene for wrinkled seeds he called *recessive.*

Humans, too, have pairs of genes that help determine different traits. If a person has genes with different directions for the same trait, one of the genes is dominant and the other is recessive. But human genetics is much more complicated than the genetics of pea plants. For example, skin color in humans is controlled by at least six pairs of

GENETIC PLANNING

Plant genetics
The first Delicious apples were of mixed yellow and red color. When a particular branch produced all-red apples, fruit growers grafted parts of that branch to other trees. By grafting over and over, they developed whole trees that produced red Delicious apples.

genes. Your hair color, eye color, and height are also controlled by many pairs of genes.

Some living things are *hybrids.* A hybrid can be created by parents of different varieties of a species. For example, a mule is a hybrid. A mule can be created only by the mating of a horse and a donkey. Like some other hybrids, mules cannot reproduce by mating with each other.

Plant scientists have learned much about plant hybrids. They have created new fruits and vegetables by "mixing" different varieties. They have also created new varieties of wheat, corn, and other important crops so that these will grow well in particular climates and soils. (*See* **plant breeding.**)

Genes and Disease Certain human medical problems are inherited. For example, diabetes is an inherited disease that makes a person's body have trouble using sugar properly. Color blindness is another inherited problem. A color-blind person does not see colors the way most people see them. Hemophilia, another inherited disease, prevents a person's blood from clotting properly.

Inherited medical problems are related to chemicals the body produces. The body makes these chemicals by following the instructions it finds in genes. Sometimes, a

When a pea plant has one gene for smooth seeds and one for wrinkled seeds, it produces three smooth seeds for every wrinkled seed. The gene for smooth seeds is *dominant.*

Animal genetics
Animal growers developed improved kinds of animals by selective breeding — such as cows that give more milk, and hogs that have less fat. Now, using genetic engineering, we have crossed a goat and a sheep to produce a *geep* — an animal with wool like a sheep and a face like a goat.

person has genes with the wrong instructions for making a certain chemical. Things may go wrong in that person's body. For example, growth hormone is a chemical that makes humans grow. A few children cannot make this chemical because there is something wrong with their genetic instructions for it.

Scientists have learned how to put the gene for human growth hormone into bacteria. The bacteria follow the instructions in the gene and make human growth hormone. This chemical can be collected from the bacteria and given to children who cannot make their own growth hormone. These children can then grow normally.

Genetic Engineering Taking genes from one living thing and putting them into another living thing is part of a science called *genetic engineering*. Scientists hope that they will someday be able to cure many inherited problems by using genetic engineering. They want to be able to give a child who cannot make growth hormone a healthy gene for this chemical. If they succeed, the child will be able to make the hormone in his or her own body instead of taking it like a medicine.

Scientists see many other uses for genetic engineering. It could be used to make better food plants, such as wheat and corn. These plants might grow faster, produce more food, and be less likely to be damaged by insects. Genetic engineering might also be used to make trees that have stronger wood, or cotton plants with more cotton fibers.

See also **heredity.**

Genghis Khan

Genghis Khan (JEN-gis KAHN or GENG-is KAHN) was one of the greatest conquerers the world has ever known. By the time he died, in 1227, the empire he had created stretched all the way across Asia.

Genghis Khan was born around the year 1162 in Mongolia. His real name was Temujin, which means "ironsmith." Temujin's father was the head of one of Mongolia's many tribes. After his father died, Temujin became the leader. He was only 13 years old, but he proved he was strong enough to lead. He soon united all the tribes of Mongolia. In 1206, he was given the title Genghis Khan—"Perfect Warrior."

Genghis Khan first took his Mongols into part of China, which they conquered. He then led his forces west across the plains of

Genghis Khan, a Mongol warrior, conquered a huge empire around the year 1200.

central Asia to Iran. The armies of Genghis Khan also invaded parts of northern India, Russia, and Afghanistan.

The Mongols showed no mercy to their enemies. But they could also be fair. For example, they let people continue to practice their own religions.

When Genghis Khan died, his empire was divided among his four sons. The Mongols continued to rule a huge territory in Asia until the middle 1300s.

geodesic dome

A geodesic dome is a building shaped like a ball or an upside-down bowl. It is formed by a skeleton of triangles. The sides of the triangles are straight. But each triangle is placed at a slightly different angle than all the other triangles it touches. This gives the structure a rounded shape and great strength. The weight of the dome is spread evenly throughout the triangles. No inside supporting beams are needed. A lightweight building material covers the skeleton.

The United States pavilion for Expo '67 in Montreal, Canada, is a geodesic dome. It towers above the trees, and looks like a gigantic golden ball.

The space inside a geodesic dome cannot easily be divided into separate rooms. Floor-to-ceiling walls would block airflow and make temperature control difficult. Instead, walls half the height of the dome are used to create "rooms."

The geodesic dome was invented by R. Buckminster Fuller, an architect and designer. He believed geodesic domes were suitable for houses, factories, and sports arenas. Fuller once proposed constructing a dome 2 miles (3.2 kilometers) in diameter over New York City. He believed the climate inside such a dome could be controlled to create ideal living conditions.

See also **architecture.**

The triangles in a geodesic dome help make it strong. At left, the triangles are bars to climb on. Below, some of the triangle spaces in a geodesic house are windows.

geography

Geography is the study of lands and places on earth. Geographers are interested in many things. Some geographers study the shape and size of the land itself. Others study where people live and how they use the land. Some study which plants and animals live in different regions.

The most important tools of geography are maps. They can show many things. Physical maps show the location of mountains and rivers. Other maps show how different countries or states fit together and where cities, towns, and highways are.

There are maps that show where forests grow, where farmers raise crops, and even where birds travel in the spring and fall. Weather maps show what the weather is like in a particular region. (*See* **map.**)

Geography can be broken into several parts. *Physical geography* is the study of the land itself. Physical geographers want to know where to find the highest mountains, the longest rivers, and the driest deserts.

Social geography is the study of people on the land. Social geographers want to know where people live and why. Why do so many people live near oceans and lakes? Why did people build a city in one spot rather than another?

Social geographers also ask why people around the world live so differently from one another. Why do they dress differently, eat different kinds of foods, and have so many different customs?

Economic geography studies how people use the land's resources. Some regions have rich soil for growing food. Some regions have important metals or oil under the ground. Cities often grow up at important crossroads, because many people come there to buy and sell goods.

Geography is useful to many people. We use maps to find our way when we travel, or to learn about a region of the world. Geographers help plan new shopping centers, new roads, and new cities. (*See* **city.**)

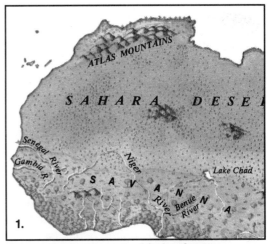

Geographers use many kinds of maps. Map 1 shows the land—mountains, rivers, and deserts. Maps 2 and 3 tell about people. Map 2 shows the borders of countries, and 3 shows where the most people live.

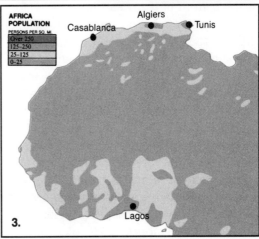

geology

Geology is one of several earth sciences. It deals with the solid part of the earth. Other earth sciences include *meteorology*—the study of weather; *oceanography*—the study of the oceans; and *hydrology*—the study of water. Scientists who study geology are called *geologists.*

Geologists work mostly with the different kinds of rocks and minerals that make up the earth's crust. Some geologists are mainly interested in understanding how the earth is made. Others are *economic geologists.* Economic geologists are interested in finding new deposits of minerals from which we can get useful things like metals and chemicals. They also search for new deposits of fuels such as oil, gas, and coal.

Geologists make maps showing the different kinds of rocks they have found in an area. These maps tell them much about the geologic history of the area. When the histories of many areas are pieced together, geologists can even describe the changes that an entire continent has undergone over millions of years. *Paleontologists,* scientists who study the fossilized remains of ancient life, help geologists figure out how old rocks are. They also help to match the rocks of one area with another. (*See* **fossil.**)

Oceanographers, too, work closely with geologists—and may also be geologists themselves. The study of the rocks and minerals at the bottom of the ocean is really geology. But scientists who do such studies often think of themselves as oceanographers.

One of the things geologists study is the way mountains are formed. Some mountains have risen because of movements in the earth's crust. Other mountains may have been the result of one continent colliding with another. Geologists know that the Himalayas and the Alps were formed that way. (*See* **Himalayas** and **Alps.**)

Other mountains, such as volcanoes, rise because of activity in the deep region of the earth called the *mantle.* (*See* **volcano.**)

Some geologists study the shock waves that happen when the slowly moving plates of the earth's crust give a sudden lurch. (*See* **earthquake.**)

See also **Earth; earth history; continental drift; rock;** and **mineral.**

geometry

Geometry is the part of mathematics that deals with points, lines, and shapes. The word *geometry* comes from Greek words that mean "to measure earth." Ancient people needed to measure distances, fields, and rivers. They needed to know which angles to use when building pyramids. The rules of geometry helped them find answers to these puzzles.

GEOMETRIC FIGURES

A *plane figure,* such as a square, has height and width. A *solid figure,* such as a cube, has height, width, and depth.

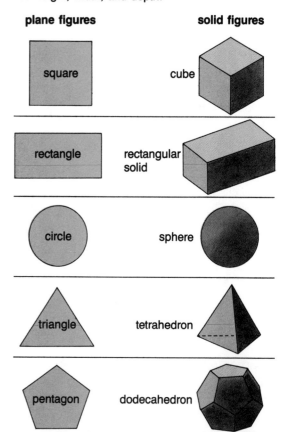

plane figures	solid figures
square	cube
rectangle	rectangular solid
circle	sphere
triangle	tetrahedron
pentagon	dodecahedron

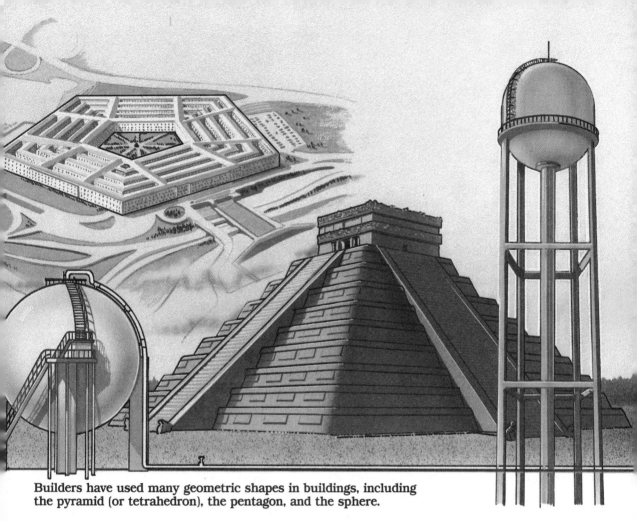

Builders have used many geometric shapes in buildings, including the pyramid (or tetrahedron), the pentagon, and the sphere.

The triangle, square, rectangle, and pentagon are geometric shapes drawn with lines that meet at their endpoints. A triangle has three sides, a square and a rectangle have four, and a pentagon has five.

Geometric shapes can also be drawn with curves. A circle is a closed curve. All the points on the curve are the same distance from the center of the circle.

Not all geometric shapes are flat. Some are solid. A cube is a solid figure, like a block. A sphere is a ball. A cylinder is the same shape as an orange juice can.

Greek mathematicians began studying these simple figures around 600 B.C. They were able to prove that geometric figures follow certain rules. For example, any triangle that has two sides of equal length also has two angles of equal measure. A Greek mathematician named Euclid put these rules together in a book called *The Elements.*

After Euclid, much progress in geometry came as people tried to solve three famous problems. The first problem was to find a cube that has twice the volume of a given cube. The second was to find a square with the area of a circle. The third was to divide an angle into three equal parts.

These problems may not sound very hard to solve. But there was a catch—only two tools were to be used to solve the problems. One tool, the straightedge, is like a ruler without marks. The other tool was a compass, used for drawing circles. Trying to solve these problems led mathematicians to discover properties of more complicated shapes, such as spirals and ellipses. But by the 1900s, it was shown that none of these problems could be solved with a straightedge and compass.

Geometry is very important to us today. We use the rules of geometry for building bridges, skyscrapers, and roads. We use geometry when we launch rockets and plan their re-entry to earth.

See also **mathematics** and **measurement.**

Georgia

Capital: Atlanta
Area: 58,910 square miles (152,577 square kilometers) (21st-largest state)
Population (1980): 5,464,265 (1985): about 5,976,000 (11th-largest state)
Became a state: January 2, 1788 (4th state)

Georgia is the largest state east of the Mississippi River. On a map, it looks a little like a nose, with its eastern tip touching the Atlantic Ocean. South Carolina lies to the north, and Florida to the south.

Land Northern Georgia is mountainous. The Appalachian Mountains are in the northwest. The Blue Ridge Mountains are in the northeast. The highest peak in the state has the colorful name of Brasstown Bald. It is 4,784 feet (1,458 meters) high and is in the Blue Ridge Mountains.

Southern Georgia is flat. Parts of it are swampy or marshy. The Okefenokee is the second-largest natural swamp in the United States. Only Florida's Everglades is larger. Some 681 square miles (1,764 square kilometers) of the Okefenokee is in Georgia. The rest is in Florida. *Okefenokee* means "trembling earth." The Indians named it well, because what seems to be land is actually spongy mats of plants that tremble when you walk on them.

Alligators are among the many animals that live in the Okefenokee. An alligator's roar is louder than a lion's. Every time a jet thunders over the Okefenokee, the alligators answer with thunder of their own.

Georgia has a warm, moist climate, with mild winters. Cotton is a major crop, but Georgia is also known for peanuts and peaches. It ranks first among the states in growing peanuts and third in peaches.

We get more granite from Georgia than from any other state. The world's largest exposed block of granite is Stone Mountain, near the city of Atlanta. Stone Mountain is 683 feet (208 meters) tall and 1½ miles (2.4 kilometers) long.

History The Spanish explorer Hernando de Soto came looking for gold in 1539, but did not find any. Other Spaniards tried to colonize Georgia, but the Indians drove them away. No European settlements survived until the English arrived in 1733. Georgia was the last colony in America to be settled by the English. When the English arrived, they found Cherokee Indians in the north and Creek Indians in the south. The Cherokees were very advanced. By 1828 they had their own weekly newspaper, published in the Cherokee language. But white settlers forced both the Creek and the Cherokee to leave their homes and go to what is now the state of Oklahoma. (*See* **Indians, American.**)

Georgia was the last of the English colonies to join the American Revolution. Cotton became "king" in Georgia after the Revolution, especially after Eli Whitney invented the cotton gin in 1793. Black slaves worked on the large plantations. (*See* **slavery** and **Whitney, Eli.**)

During the Civil War, Georgia joined the Confederate States of America. The Confederate Army won two important battles in Georgia. But in September 1864, the Northern general William T. Sherman captured and burned Atlanta. Then he and his troops marched across Georgia to Savannah. Along the way, they killed, burned, or stole anything they could. It took the state many years to recover from the damage. (*See* **Civil War.**)

People Georgia's economy used to be mainly agricultural, but it is becoming more industrial. Manufacturing textiles is now a more important industry than growing cotton. One of the world's largest peanut-butter factories is in Dawson, Georgia.

Most Georgians live in cities now, because that is where the industries are. Atlanta,

16

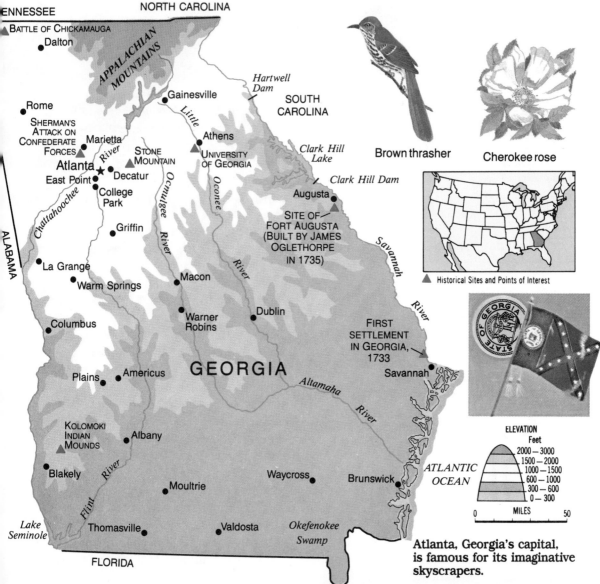

TENNESSEE

NORTH CAROLINA

▲ BATTLE OF CHICKAMAUGA

● Dalton

APPALACHIAN MOUNTAINS

● Rome

SHERMAN'S ATTACK ON CONFEDERATE FORCES ▲ Marietta

● Gainesville

Hartwell Dam

SOUTH CAROLINA

Little River

● Athens
▲ UNIVERSITY OF GEORGIA

Clark Hill Lake

STONE MOUNTAIN ▲

Atlanta ★

Decatur ●

East Point ●

● College Park

Clark Hill Dam

Augusta ▲

Chattahoochee River

Ocmulgee River

Oconee River

Savannah River

● Griffin

SITE OF FORT AUGUSTA (BUILT BY JAMES OGLETHORPE IN 1735)

ALABAMA

● La Grange

● Warm Springs

● Macon

River

● Dublin

FIRST SETTLEMENT IN GEORGIA, 1733

● Columbus

● Warner Robins

GEORGIA

Savannah

Altamaha River

● Plains ● Americus

KOLOMOKI INDIAN MOUNDS ▲

● Albany

● Blakely

River

Flint River

● Moultrie

Waycross ●

Brunswick ●

ATLANTIC OCEAN

Lake Seminole

● Thomasville

● Valdosta

Okefenokee Swamp

FLORIDA

Brown thrasher

Cherokee rose

Historical Sites and Points of Interest ▲

ELEVATION
Feet
2000 – 3000
1500 – 2000
1000 – 1500
600 – 1000
300 – 600
0 – 300

0   MILES   50

Atlanta, Georgia's capital, is famous for its imaginative skyscrapers.

Georgia's capital, has about 436,200 people, and is Georgia's largest manufacturing center. It is also the distribution and transportation center for all of the southeastern United States. (*See* **Atlanta**.)

Savannah was the first town in the state, so it is called the "Mother City of Georgia." Savannah is an important seaport on the Atlantic Ocean. It is also the home of the largest paper mill in the world.

Jimmy Carter, the 39th President of the United States, is from Georgia. The Carters are peanut farmers from the town of Plains. Another famous Georgian was Martin Luther King, Jr., the civil-rights leader.

gerbil, *see* **hamsters and gerbils**

Germany

WEST GERMANY		
Capital: Bonn		
Area: 95,976 square miles (248,578 square kilometers)		
Population (1985): about 60,950,000		
Official language: German		
EAST GERMANY		
Capital: East Berlin		
Area: 41,768 square miles (108,179 square kilometers)		
Population (1985): about 16,686,000		
Official language: German		

Germany is not one country, but two—West Germany and East Germany. They are neighbors in central Europe. West Germany's official name is the Federal Republic of Germany. East Germany's official name is the German Democratic Republic.

West Germany is the larger of the two nations. It has about as much land as the state of Wyoming. East Germany has only about half as much. Many more people live in West Germany.

The two countries have very different kinds of government. In West Germany, the people elect their officials, and individuals own and operate most of the large businesses. East Germany has a communist government. The government owns the large businesses and controls how people live. West Germany is friendly with France, Britain, and the United States. East Germany is friendly with the Soviet Union.

Land The land of the two Germanys stretches from the Baltic Sea in the north to high mountains called the Alps in the south. Moving from north to south is like climbing giant stairs. The northern regions of the two countries are flat lowlands. The central region has rolling hills and small mountains. The southern part of West Germany is high in the Alps.

Several of Germany's large cities are in the north. Berlin, in northern East Germany is a special city. For many years, it was the capital of one Germany. Today, it is like Germany itself, divided into an eastern and a western half. (*See* **Berlin.**)

Frankfurt (left) is an important West German city on the Main River. Leipzig, East Germany (right), is world famous for its trade shows.

In West Germany, many large cities lie near the Rhine River. The valley of the Ruhr River, which flows into the Rhine, is West Germany's center of manufacturing. The major river in East Germany is the Elbe.

A third large river, the Danube, runs through southern Germany. It begins in the Black Forest, a land of rolling hills and dark evergreen trees.

History For hundreds of years, Germany was made up of many independent cities and small states.

In the early 1500s, a German monk named Martin Luther began criticizing some practices of the Roman Catholic Church. One of the things he said was that people should read the Bible in their own language. He translated the whole Bible into German. German became an important language, read and spoken by millions of people.

In 1871, the people of Germany were united into a single strong country. Germans were proud of their country. They had many writers and musicians. They also had many factories and strong armies.

But German leaders wanted more land, and they tried to take it from Germany's neighbors. In 1914, Germany and Austria attacked France, Britain, and Russia in World War I. Germany lost the war, and some of its territory was taken away. In the years that followed, Germany's government was weak, and the Nazi party took over, headed by Adolf Hitler. In 1939, Hitler's armies invaded Poland and France, starting World War II. Again, Germany was defeated. The United States fought against Germany in both wars. (*See* **World War I; World War II;** and **Hitler, Adolf.**)

World War II destroyed much of Germany. When the war ended, in 1945, the winning countries agreed to help govern and rebuild Germany. The Soviet Union controlled the eastern part of the country. The United States, Britain, and France controlled the western part.

In 1949, the three nations that controlled western Germany wanted to make the country independent again. But the Soviet Union did not want its portion to be part of the new Germany. Because of this disagreement, Germany became two countries: West Germany and East Germany.

People Germans have made important contributions to science, music, and literature. Albert Einstein, one of the great scientists of the 1900s, was German. So was Karl Benz, who built the first gasoline-powered car in the late 1800s. (*See* **Einstein, Albert** and **automobile.**)

Germany has produced some of the greatest composers of music. They include Johann Sebastian Bach and Ludwig van Beethoven. There have been many great German writers, such as Johann Wolfgang von Goethe and Thomas Mann. The Grimm Brothers studied the German language and collected fairy tales.

Today, the two Germanys are important European countries. Despite the many differences between them, the two Germanys have a history and culture in common. They are trying to improve their relationship. They sometimes work together on special projects that will help both, such as road construction.

Geronimo

Geronimo was a leader of the Apache Indians who fought against the Mexicans and American settlers during the 1800s. Geronimo's Indian name was *Goyathlay.* The name Geronimo, which is Spanish for "Jerome," was given to him by the Mexicans.

Geronimo was born in 1829 in what is today New Mexico. At that time, the Apaches lived in an area that included parts of present-day Mexico, Arizona, and New Mexico. In 1858, while on a trading trip to Mexico, Geronimo's mother, wife, and children were killed by Mexican soldiers. Swearing revenge, Geronimo led many bloody raids against the Mexicans over the years.

During this time, white settlers in the United States were pushing farther west and taking over Indian lands. The government forced the Indians to move to lands called *reservations.* Geronimo and his followers escaped from reservations several times. They attacked American and Mexican settlements during the 1870s and 1880s, trying to force the settlers out.

Geronimo surrendered to the U.S. Army in 1886. By then, he was famous. He lived on the reservation at Fort Sill, Oklahoma until his death in 1909.

See also **Indian Wars.**

Geronimo led one of the last Indian battles against the United States.

George Gershwin writes one of his songs at the piano.

Gershwin, George

George Gershwin composed music for movies, concerts, and Broadway shows. He wrote many popular songs, but also wrote symphonies, and even a famous opera.

Gershwin was born in 1898 and grew up in Brooklyn, New York. He was more interested in sports than in music until he heard a schoolmate play the violin. After that, George began taking piano lessons.

He got a job as a pianist when he was only 16. He also began to write his own music. His first hit song, "Swanee," made him famous before he was 21.

In 1924, Gershwin wrote *Rhapsody in Blue,* a showy concert piece for piano and orchestra. The *Rhapsody* surprised people with its modern melodies and jazz rhythms. (*See* **jazz.**)

Also in 1924, Gershwin wrote a musical comedy called *Lady, Be Good.* His brother Ira wrote the *lyrics*—the words for the music. Together, the two brothers wrote many more popular musicals.

In 1935, Gershwin wrote the opera *Porgy and Bess.* It was about poor black people, and Gershwin used jazz and "the blues" kinds of music that blacks first developed. Many of the songs from *Porgy and Bess* are still favorites today.

Gershwin died in 1937, when he was only 39. He is still one of America's most beloved composers.

Gettysburg

The battle of Gettysburg was one of the bloodiest battles of the Civil War and the greatest one ever fought on United States soil. The fighting took place over the southern Pennsylvania countryside for three days, from July 1 to July 3, 1863.

Since the start of the Civil War in 1861, most of the battles had been fought in the South. In June of 1863, the commander of the Confederate forces, General Robert E. Lee, decided to march his army of 75,000 soldiers north into Pennsylvania to attack the Union army. Lee believed that a victory on northern soil would accomplish two things. Confederate troops would be able to find badly needed supplies such as food and weapons in the North. Also, a Southern victory might frighten the North into talking about peace. By the end of June 1863, Lee's soldiers had marched through Maryland and into Pennsylvania. Following them was a Union force of almost 90,000 led by General George B. Meade.

On the morning of July 1, parts of both the Union and the Confederate armies were scattered over the area surrounding the town of Gettysburg. Neither side was prepared to do battle there. The fighting began almost by accident when Union soldiers on horseback surprised a group of Confederate soldiers who were in Gettysburg looking for supplies.

On the first day of the battle, both sides tried to find the best positions for fighting. The Union army settled in the hills south of Gettysburg. Lee's soldiers made their camp on a ridge to the west. On the second day, Confederate forces made several attacks on the Union lines, but were driven back each time. Finally, on the third day, Lee ordered General George Pickett to lead 15,000 men directly into the center of the Union forces. Pickett lost almost two-thirds of his soldiers as they charged across an open field and into the gunfire of the Union Army. Lee then admitted defeat and led his army back

Union cannons fire at charging Confederate soldiers during Pickett's charge. The Confederates were driven back, and soon had to retreat from Gettysburg.

South. The exhausted Union troops did not even have the energy to pursue them.

During the battle of Gettysburg, almost 18,000 Union soldiers and more than 20,000 Confederate soldiers were either killed or wounded. The following November, President Abraham Lincoln came to Gettysburg to dedicate the cemetery where the fallen soldiers were buried. There he gave a short speech that is still famous today—the Gettysburg Address.

See also **Civil War; Lee, Robert E.;** and **Lincoln, Abraham.**

geyser

A geyser (GUY-zer) is an underground spring that shoots boiling-hot water and steam up out of the earth.

Hot rock deep within the earth's crust heats water that has trickled down from the surface through deep cracks. The hot water begins rising back up through other cracks. When the water reaches boiling temperature, part of it changes to steam. The steam and water explode up out of the ground. Sometimes geysers may rise as high as 60 meters (197 feet).

Some geysers erupt at regular intervals day after day. Old Faithful geyser in Yellowstone National Park has been erupting about once an hour for more than 80 years.

Almost all the world's geysers are located in the western United States, Iceland, and New Zealand. In California and New Zealand, the heat from geysers is harnessed to make electricity.

A geyser at Yellowstone shoots steam and hot water high into the air.

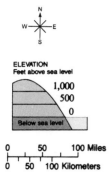

ELEVATION
Feet above sea level

1,000
500
0
Below sea level

0   50   100 Miles
0   50   100 Kilometers

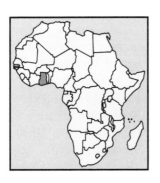

Ghana

Capital: Accra	
Area: 92,099 square miles (238,536 square kilometers)	
Population (1985): about 13,004,000	
Official language: English	

Ghana is a West African country located along the Gulf of Guinea. A former colony of Great Britain, Ghana was once known as the *Gold Coast* because of the large amounts of gold found there. When the Gold Coast became independent in 1957, it was renamed

Ghana after an ancient black African kingdom. (*See* **African civilizations.**)

Most of the people of Ghana are black. About 50 different languages are spoken, but English is the official language.

Northern Ghana is very dry, and most people live in the south. Accra, the capital, and Tema, the largest port, are both located on the southern coast. A dam across the Volta River near Tema provides electricity. The dam also created Lake Volta, one of the world's largest man-made lakes.

Lumbermen in Ghana use a power saw to cut apart a giant log.

Lumbering and mining are important industries. Ghana is rich in gold, diamonds, and manganese. But most Ghanaians make their living as farmers. Ghana's most important crop is cocoa beans, which are used to make chocolate.

ghost

A ghost is the spirit of a dead person that comes back to earth. In the past, most people believed in ghosts. Sometimes they hoped to meet the ghost of a friend or a family member, but often they were afraid of ghosts. Today, most people do not believe that a dead person can return as a ghost. They think that the idea of ghosts comes from people's imaginations.

There are many stories about ghosts. One is that a dead person's ghost comes back to a house where he or she lived and stays there. A house that is supposed to have a ghost is called a *haunted* house.

According to the stories, many ghosts are peaceful, but a few of them are noisy and violent. A *poltergeist* is a ghost or spirit who can throw things across a room or shake dishes off a shelf.

In the story *A Christmas Carol,* the miserly Scrooge is visited by several ghosts. This one is the ghost of his dead business partner Jacob Marley.

In many poems and stories, ghosts come back from the dead to remind people of something important.

Today, many people like to have fun with the idea of ghosts. They may dress up as a ghost for Halloween or tell spooky stories about ghosts to tease their friends.

giant

A giant is a very big person. People can grow into giants if their pituitary gland makes too much hormone. The hormone makes the bones keep growing. (*See* **hormone.**)

In fairy tales and myths, giants are not human beings. Instead, they are an imaginary race of tall, strong creatures. Giants are also mentioned in the Bible. The giant Goliath

In "Jack and the Beanstalk," Jack climbs the beanstalk and visits a giant's house. While the giant is asleep, Jack carries away a hen that lays golden eggs.

was killed by a stone thrown from a sling by young David. (*See* **David.**)

Giants appear in Greek, Roman, and Norse myths. The giants of Greek and Roman myths were called *Titans.* The *jotnar* were the Norse giants. In the myths, giants existed before the gods. But when the gods became powerful, they conquered the giants. In the *Odyssey*, a Greek epic poem, the hero Odysseus must escape from Polyphemus, one of the one-eyed giants called Cyclops. (*See* **Homer.**)

In fairy tales, giants are often evil or stupid. The giant in the famous English tale "Jack the Giant-Killer" threatens to eat Jack. But in some stories, giants are helpful. American folklore tells of the giant Paul Bunyan and his blue ox, Babe. They use their enormous size and strength to do amazing feats. (*See* **Bunyan, Paul.**)

giraffe

Giraffes are the tallest animals on earth. A male giraffe may grow to be 5 meters (17 feet) tall and weigh more than one ton. Females are smaller. One-third of a giraffe's height is its long neck. Yet the giraffe has only seven neck bones—exactly the same number that you have!

A giraffe also has very long legs. The front legs look longer than the back legs, but all four legs are really the same length. The feet are protected by hard hoofs. The hoofs make it possible for the giraffe to run over rough ground. A giraffe can run 48 kilometers (30 miles) per hour. At this speed, lions and other predators cannot catch it. If a predator does get too close, the giraffe will kick.

Giraffes have a pair of horns on their heads. The horns are covered with skin and are never shed. The horns of males are longer and thicker than the horns of females. Giraffes may grow more hornlike bumps on their heads as they age.

Giraffes are plant-eaters. They eat mostly leaves from trees and bushes. A giraffe wraps its long tongue around the leaves and pulls them into its mouth. Sometimes, a giraffe eats grass. It has to spread its front legs wide apart so its head can reach the ground. It also stands this way when it drinks from a river or lake.

Giraffes live in Africa. They live in grasslands and along the edge of forests. Their brown-and-cream spotted coats blend into the background, hiding the giraffes from their main enemy, the lion. No two giraffes

Giraffes are fast runners, even though they look clumsy when they run.

have exactly the same coat pattern. This makes it easier for scientists who study giraffes to identify an animal from one year to the next.

A female giraffe usually gives birth to one baby at a time. A newborn giraffe is taller than most adult humans! It is about 180 centimeters (6 feet) tall and weighs about 60 kilograms (130 pounds). It is able to stand on its thin legs within an hour of its birth. Several hours later, it is able to walk and even to run.

Girl Scouts

The Girl Scouts of America is an organization that girls join to have fun, learn about their world, and help their communities. In many countries, including Canada, similar groups are called Girl Guides.

The Girl Scouts has five age levels. Very young girls may become Daisy Girl Scouts when they are 5 or 6 years old. Brownies are 6 to 8 years old. At age 8, Brownies may become Junior Girl Scouts, and are Juniors until age 11. Between the ages of 11 and 14, they are Cadette Girl Scouts. The oldest group is the Senior Girl Scouts, who are 14 to 17.

Scouts are taught how to help others, and community service is an important part of scouting. Camping and learning about the outdoors are favorite Scout activities. Arts and crafts, music, dance, and other creative activities may be part of scouting, too. As Scouts master skills, they earn badges. They wear the badges on their uniforms.

Robert Baden-Powell and his sister, Agnes Baden-Powell, started the Girl Guides in Great Britain in 1909. (Robert had earlier started the Boy Scouts.) Juliette Gordon Low started Girl Guides in the United States in 1912. Later, the name was changed to Girl Scouts.

Girl Scouts of America and Girl Guides of Canada belong to a world organization. It has meeting places in England, Switzerland, Mexico, and India.

glacier

A glacier is a large body of ice that slowly moves downhill. As glaciers move, they cause major changes in the shape of the land they cross.

About three-quarters of the earth's fresh water is frozen as glacial ice. Glaciers are found in high, mountainous regions and in the Antarctic. The vast sheets of floating ice that cover much of the Arctic Ocean are *ice floes.* Glaciers form only on land.

In Antarctica and Greenland, many glaciers have come together to form a thick blanket covering thousands of square miles. We call such a giant glacier an *ice sheet.* Ice sheets move outward in all directions. Most of the world's glacial ice is in the Antarctic ice sheet. But thousands of years ago, during the periods called *ice ages,* giant ice sheets also covered large areas of North America, Europe, and Asia. (*See* ice age.)

Today, there are glaciers in all of the world's highest mountain ranges. Compared to ice sheets, these glaciers are relatively small. Many are only a few miles long. But there are tens of thousands of them. Some of the longest mountain glaciers are in Alaska. One, the Hubbard Glacier, is over 100 kilometers (62 miles) long.

Mountain glaciers flow down narrow, steep-walled valleys. They may move as much as a meter (3 feet) in a day, but many move more slowly. The moving glacier picks up chunks of rock, which become frozen into the glacier. This rock makes the glacier act like a giant piece of sandpaper. As it slowly moves down the valley, it erodes the rocky walls and floor by grinding and scratching them.

The ice at the bottom and sides of a glacier flows more slowly than the ice at the top and in the middle. This causes the ice to pull apart, forming cracks called *crevasses.* Crevasses may be as deep as 30 meters (98 feet) and hundreds of meters long. When new snow hides them, they are a danger to mountain climbers.

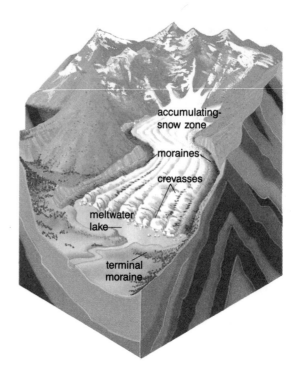

As the ice moves slowly downhill, it forms piles of rock and gravel called *moraines.*

When you sand a piece of wood, you make sawdust. When a glacier does this to rock, it makes rock fragments of all different sizes. Some are as large as boulders. Others are so small that together they form rock powder. A deposit of all these fragments is called *till.*

Water from melting ice comes pouring out of the front end of a glacier. This glacial water carries with it a load of till. Where the water leaves the ice, it drops its load of till. The till piles up to form a hill called a *kame.*

During ice ages, streams of water poured out all along the edges of the great ice sheets. In places, the kames joined together, forming *outwash plains.* Long Island, at the southern end of New York State, is what remains of an outwash plain. Long Island is almost 190 kilometers (120 miles) long and up to 30 kilometers (20 miles) wide.

Glacier National Park

Glacier National Park is in northwest Montana, near the Canadian border. The park was named for the over 50 *glaciers*—long,

The ice of the Athabasca Glacier in Canada flows slowly down the mountainside. At the bottom is the *terminal moraine*—the rock and gravel piled up by the glacier.

narrow sheets of ice—that cover the slopes of the mountains there. The area was made a national park in 1910. It attracts more than 2 million visitors each year. The park was united with the nearby Waterton Lakes National Park in Canada in 1932. Together, the two parks are known as the Waterton-Glacier International Peace Park.

The rugged Lewis Range of the Rocky Mountains covers much of Glacier National Park. Its lakes, streams, rivers, and waterfalls are popular attractions. The Lewis Overthrust is a large ridge with rock layers of different colors.

The park is also known for its great variety of trees and animal life. Bears, elk, mountain goats, cougars, and moose roam the land. Hawks and eagles can often be seen flying overhead.

Glacier National Park has over 1,000 miles (1,600 kilometers) of trails. Tourists enjoy hiking, mountain climbing, horseback riding, and swimming during the summer months, when the park is open.

See also **glacier.**

gland

Glands are organs that make substances that are needed by the body. Sweat glands produce sweat, which helps cool the body and keep the skin moist. Tear glands make tears, which keep the eyes moist. Mucous glands in the mouth make saliva, which moistens food. Saliva also contains a chemical that begins the digestion of starches. Glands in the stomach and small intestine make other chemicals that the body uses to digest food.

Still other glands control many of the body's activities. The thyroid gland controls how fast the body changes food into energy. The parathyroid glands control the body's use of calcium. The pancreas is a gland that regulates the body's use of sugar. The adrenal gland controls the heartbeat rate in times of stress and excitement. It also controls the water and mineral balance in the body. The sex glands cause boys and girls to develop differently. At a certain age, boys grow beards and develop deep voices. Their

27

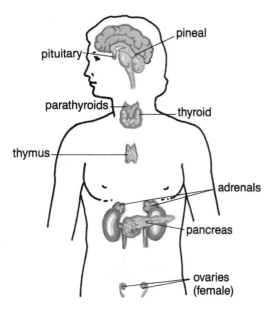

The body has important glands in
the head, chest, and abdomen.

bodies begin to produce sperm. Girls develop
breasts, and begin to produce ova—eggs
—and menstruate each month.

The pituitary is sometimes called the
"master gland," because it controls the other
glands. The pituitary also receives messages
from the hypothalamus in the brain. In this
way, the pituitary acts as a link between the
brain and the rest of the body.

See also **hormone.**

glass

Glass is made from a mixture of hot, melted
sand and small amounts of metals. Glass is
used in windows and mirrors. It is made into
bottles, light bulbs, camera lenses, Christmas ornaments, and many other things.

Glass has some special qualities. Glass
does not conduct electricity. It does not have
a melting point. Instead, it slowly softens
and melts as it is heated, and hardens as it
cools. Once cool, it is *brittle*—it will break,
but not bend. Glass is *translucent*—light can
pass through it.

Melted glass looks like thick, red-hot
syrup. The hot glass can be shaped into objects or rolled into sheets. When the glass
cools, it is usually colorless, and you can see

through it. Before the invention of plastic,
the lenses in all eyeglasses were made of
glass. Glass used for mirrors is coated on the
back, so instead of looking through the
glass, you see your reflection.

Glass can be colored by adding certain
metals to the sand. Blue glass can be made
by adding a small amount of the metal co-
balt. Adding iron can turn glass green. (*See*
stained glass.)

A problem with glass is that it can break
into pieces. For safety, an automobile's wind-
shield is a sandwich of a thin layer of plastic
between two sheets of glass. If the wind-
shield is broken, the pieces do not go flying.
They stay stuck to the plastic.

Glass can form naturally when sand is
melted by lightning or by a volcano. When
early people found pieces of this glass, they
used it to make knives and jewelry. They did
not learn to make glass themselves until
around 4000 B.C. The ancient Egyptians
used glass as a *glaze*—a thin coating—over
clay and stone beads. They began making
small, solid objects of glass around 4,500
years ago.

From a "bubble" of hot, glowing glass at
the end of the tube, this glassblower is
forming a glass container.

The Syrians may have been the first to start blowing glass, about 2,000 years ago. To blow glass, a glassblower picks up a blob of melted glass on the end of a long pipe. The glassblower blows into the other end. His or her breath fills the blob, turning it into a glass bubble. Very light, delicate bottles and vases can be made this way.

At the beginning of the 1900s, people developed machinery that could form continuous sheets of glass. Today, glass is used everywhere. Television screens are made of glass. Glass fibers are put into walls to keep houses warm in winter and cool in summer. Glass in fiber form, called *fiber glass*, is used to build boats and car bodies.

glue

Glue is a sticky substance used for holding things together. There are many kinds of glues. Some are made from animal bones, hides, or milk. Others are made from plants or from *synthetics*—materials made by people. Some glues are made to hold paper or wood together. Other glues work best on glass, metal, or plastic. Furniture and plywood are made with very strong glues. A glue made from fish bones is used on gummed stamps and labels. Wallpaper may be put up with glue made from wheat flour.

Glues made from sugar, cornstarch, wheat flour, bones, or milk are *natural glues.* Most synthetic glues are made from petroleum. Some synthetic glues do not become stiff and hard even when they dry.

Most natural glues are dissolved in water. When the water evaporates, the glue sticks and bonds. Some synthetic glues work the opposite way—they absorb moisture in order to set. Sticky tapes and bandages use waterless glues. Pressure makes them stick. Epoxy glue sets a very strong bond when two different chemicals are mixed.

CAUTION: Epoxy glues and some other synthetic glues are very strong and may harden quickly. You should be careful not to get them on your skin.

goat

ibex

Saanen

Angora

The ibex is a sure-footed mountain goat. The angora's fleece makes very fine wool. The saanen is raised for its milk.

goat

Goats are mountain animals that are found throughout the world. They are excellent rock climbers. Their hoofs help them move quickly from ledge to ledge.

The North American mountain goat is actually a sheep, not a goat. One way to tell the difference between goats and sheep is that the tails of goats point up, and the tails of sheep hang down.

Goats live in herds. Usually, they eat grass, but they may climb low trees to eat the leaves and bark. Most kinds of goats have two horns. Some male goats have beards. A male is called a *billy.* A female is called a *nanny.* Young goats are called *kids.*

People all over the world keep goats. The goats are a source of milk, meat, wool, and skins. Goatskin is used to make soft shoes and gloves. The soft fleece of cashmere goats is spun to make yarn for cashmere sweaters. The long fleece of Angora goats is the source of mohair, which is spun and used for blankets, fluffy sweaters, and other goods.

gods and goddesses

Many ancient peoples developed an advanced way of life. They built cities and traded with people of other civilizations. They taught themselves how to write and learned how to tame many animals. Still, there were forces in nature that early humans could not control or explain. Why did people get sick? What caused lightning and floods? Science gives us the answers to these questions today. Thousands of years ago, however, people believed that powerful beings—gods and goddesses—controlled nature and influenced people. Early peoples who believed in different gods made up stories about them. We call these stories *myths.*

The belief in many different gods or goddesses is called *polytheism.* Not all ancient religions had many gods or goddesses. The Hebrews believed in one God, whom they called *Yahweh.* The Egyptian ruler Akhenaton taught that of all the gods, only Aton should be worshipped.

Greek Religion The ancient Greeks felt that gods and goddesses were basically friendly. If humans were careful to honor the gods, then good things would happen. It seemed that the gods were not always fair, however. They could act out of jealousy or boredom. If a human angered the gods, trouble could occur.

To prevent this, the Greeks held festivals to honor the gods. These events often included plays, singing, praying, or sports contests, such as the Olympic Games. Each community, called a *city-state,* had its own special gods. People went to temples called *oracles.* There, they asked a priest or priestess to tell them the will of the gods.

Many Greeks learned about the gods and goddesses from the writings of the poet Homer. Homer's two great works, the *Iliad* and the *Odyssey,* describe events before and after the Trojan War. The gods and goddesses mentioned in these poems were accepted by Greeks as the most important. (*See* **Trojan War** and **Homer.**)

Apollo
god of the sun

Diana
goddess of the moon

In Greek myth, Apollo's horses pull the sun across the sky. Diana rules over the moon.

Greek Myths According to Greek myths, the gods and goddesses lived on Mount Olympus. They were ruled by Zeus, the most important and powerful of the gods. Zeus was the god of the heavens and used thunder and lightning as his weapons.

Zeus was married to Hera, the goddess of marriage. His son Apollo was the god of music, light, and poetry. Apollo played a stringed instrument called a *lyre,* which looked like a small harp. He traveled about in the chariot of the sun. Apollo's twin sister, Artemis, drove the chariot of the moon. She was the goddess of the hunt.

One Greek myth tells how Zeus gave birth to Athena. This daughter, who was the goddess of knowledge and war, was born from the head of Zeus. Aphrodite was the goddess of love. One myth states that she, too, was the daughter of Zeus. Another says she was born from sea foam. Aphrodite had a son, Eros, who was the god of love.

Hermes, another son of Zeus, was the messenger of the gods. Hermes carried a magic wand and wore sandals with wings to help him fly. A cap of darkness could make him invisible. Hermes was also the god of travelers and thieves. Part of his job was to guide souls to the underworld. Hades, the brother of Zeus, ruled the underworld.

The goddess Hestia ruled the *hearth,* the place in a home where the fire was kept. She came to be the goddess of the family.

Greek myths also included lesser gods and goddesses. Among these were the *nymphs* —beautiful girls who guarded the things of nature. Two groups of nymphs were the *nereids*—water spirits—and the *dryads*—tree spirits.

Other lesser goddesses included the nine *muses,* who ruled over the arts and sciences. The *fates* were thought to be three sisters. One spun out the thread of a person's life. The second decided how long the thread— the life—should be. The third fate was in charge of cutting the thread, thereby ending the person's life.

Roman Gods and Goddesses The ancient Romans, too, believed in many gods and goddesses. The Romans, who conquered Greece, were greatly influenced by Greek ideas and ways. As a result, Roman myths about gods and goddesses are similar to those of the Greeks. At first, the Romans worshipped three main gods. After coming into contact with the Greeks, they came to believe that one main god, Jupiter, was above the others. Like Zeus, Jupiter ruled over all. Mars was the Roman god of war. Juno was the wife of Jupiter, and Minerva was the goddess of wisdom.

See also **myths and legends** and **mythical creatures.**

Jupiter

Vulcan

Minerva

Mars

Neptune

DAYS OF THE WEEK NAMED FOR GODS AND GODDESSES

Day	Named for
Sunday	(the sun or the sun god)
Monday	(the moon or the moon god)
Tuesday	Tiu, Norse god of war, son of Odin
Wednesday	Odin, or Woden, most powerful of the Norse gods
Thursday	Thor, Norse god of thunder
Friday	Frigg, Norse goddess of love, wife of Odin
Saturday	Saturn, Roman god of feasting and fertility

This gold fan was found in the tomb of the Egyptian pharaoh Tutankhamen.

gold

Gold is one of the elements. It is a shiny yellow metal that people have used and valued for thousands of years. It is not only beautiful but soft enough to be molded into shapes. Gold does not *corrode*—rust—like other metals. It is the most popular metal for fine jewelry. It has also been used as money.

Gold was probably one of the first metals people discovered. Stone Age people wore gold nuggets as jewelry. People learned to hammer the gold into delicate shapes. More than 5,000 years ago, in what is now Iraq, kings and queens were buried with beautiful gold pieces. These pieces included cups, jewelry, and headdresses, and gold-covered harps, chariots, and helmets. The ancient Egyptians were skilled goldsmiths. They, too, buried gold objects with their dead. The mummy case of Tutankhamen was made of gold. (*See* **Tutankhamen.**)

People have searched all over the earth for gold. The Spanish conquistadores explored South America, Mexico, and what is now the southwestern part of the United States looking for gold. Gold rushes brought people to California and Alaska.

Small amounts of gold are everywhere on the earth. But more of the earth's gold is in the sea than on the land. Gold is mined from the earth and collected from streams. The largest deposits of gold are in South Africa, the Soviet Union, Canada, and the United States.

Gold does not combine easily with other elements. But other metals must be added to gold to make it hard. The purity of gold is measured in *karats.* Pure gold is 24 karats. Jewelers often use 18-karat gold, which is three-fourths gold. (*See* **alloy.**)

Gold has many uses. Dentists sometimes use gold for fillings because gold will not rust or crumble away. The glass of an astronaut's helmet is coated with gold because gold reflects damaging infrared light rays. Gold is a good conductor of heat and electricity and is used in electronic equipment.

Gold can also be hammered into a very thin film called *gold leaf.* The gold leaf is used to decorate paintings, picture frames, furniture, and even the roofs and domes of buildings. Gold leaf stays shiny, even when it is outdoors in rain and sun.

Because we are so fond of gold, we use the word *golden* to describe good things—such as a "golden opportunity" and the "golden years."

See also **element** and **metal.**

goldfish

Goldfish are the most popular fish for home aquariums. Pet goldfish are domestic animals. But goldfish that live in the wild do not look like the colorful goldfish in aquariums. They are a dull brown color. Once in a while, some wild goldfish are born as partial *albinos.* Their skin is missing all color except red. (*See* **albino.**)

Some people keep goldfish in outdoor pools. Where winters are cold, the pools must be deep enough so that not all the water freezes. The goldfish spend the winter deep in the pools. They do not move around or eat much during this time.

comet

nymph

scaleless veiltail

lionhead

Goldfish are peaceful animals. They will not fight with one another. But it is important not to put too many fish in one pool or aquarium. Overcrowding can be harmful to their health.

Hundreds of years ago, people in China caught some red goldfish and put them in ponds. When the fish reproduced, the baby fish were red, too. The Chinese made a hobby of breeding goldfish and of trying to develop new varieties. They bred fish with long fins, odd-shaped heads, or bulging eyes. Visitors to China took goldfish back to their own homelands. Today, goldfish are kept by people all over the world. Breeding goldfish to produce new varieties is still a popular hobby in China and many other countries around the world.

Some varieties look very different from the common goldfish. Goldfish come in almost any color, from pure white to dark blue or black. Some varieties, such as the shubunkin, are multicolored. Fantails and twintails have very long double tails. The celestial has large, upturned eyes. The bubble-eye has big sacs below its eyes. The lionhead has a warty "hood" on its head. Many special varieties are not as easy to raise as the common goldfish.

See also **aquarium.**

There are many beautiful varieties of goldfish. When kept in large ponds, some goldfish can grow to be two feet long.

shubunkin

celestial
telescope

black moor

pearl-scaled fantail

Gold Rush

Gold has fascinated people ever since it was first discovered in ancient times. For hundreds of years, owning gold has been a sign of wealth among people around the world. (*See* **gold.**)

News of the discovery of gold can draw thousands of people to an area. People join a gold rush in the hope that they, too, can find enough gold to become rich. Several gold rushes have taken place during the history of the United States. Over 10,000 people came to Dahlonega, Georgia, in 1828, after gold was discovered there. Thousands rushed to Colorado after gold was found near present-day Denver in 1858. But the most famous gold rush in American history happened in California in the 1840s.

John Sutter owned a large amount of land in the Sacramento Valley of California. In 1848, Sutter hired a carpenter named James Marshall to build a sawmill for him. The place chosen was along the American River, near the present-day city of Sacramento. On January 24, 1848, Marshall looked down into the stream by the mill and saw something glittering there. He brought the shiny flakes to Sutter. Their tests showed that Marshall had found gold.

News of the discovery quickly spread. People rushed to Sutter's Mill from nearby San Francisco to *prospect*—look for gold. By the end of 1848, news of the gold had traveled all over the United States and around the world.

In 1849, 80,000 gold seekers poured into California. No railroads yet crossed the United States, and the journey was very hard. The "forty-niners" got there any way they could. About half came by wagon over rugged trails across open plains and high mountains. Many prospectors made the trip

One miner pans for gold (center). He sloshes rock and gravel around in his pan until the gold sinks to the bottom. The man at the left is shoveling gravel into a "cradle."

by sailing south along the Atlantic coast, around the tip of South America, and north to California. Others sailed south as far as Panama, crossed a jungle, and then boarded a northbound ship on the Pacific coast.

Prospectors who found gold spent a lot of money. This helped the growth of cities such as San Francisco and Sacramento. Between 1848 and 1860, California's population grew from around 26,000 to 379,994 people.

Most of the forty-niners did not become wealthy. Some of them left the area, but many stayed on and became farmers. John Sutter never made a lot of money as a result of the gold rush. Gold seekers had claimed most of the gold on his land. He died a poor man in 1880.

golf

Golf is a game of skill that is popular with people of all ages. It is played on beautiful, parklike areas of land called *courses.*

A golfer drives a small, hard ball from the tee to the green, then *putts* it into the hole.

Courses are divided up into playing areas called *holes.* At one end of each hole, there is an actual hole in the ground, the *cup.* The golfer tries to hit a small, hard ball into the cup in as few tries as possible.

A golf course has either 9 or 18 holes. Play at each hole begins at a *tee,* which is located at the opposite end of the hole from the cup. The golfer uses a long, narrow club to *drive* —hit—the ball toward the cup. The *fairway* is a long stretch of cut grass that lies between the tee and the cup. The *rough* is on both sides of the fairway and has longer grass and bushes. Golfers must be careful to keep the ball on the fairway and out of the rough. Golfers must also avoid *sand traps* and ponds and streams. The *putting green* is the small, grassy area surrounding the cup.

On the green, the golfer tries to put the ball into the cup by using short, gentle strokes called *putts.*

When golfers speak of "playing a hole," they are referring to the entire area between the tee and the cup. This is generally from 100 to 600 yards (91 to 550 meters) long. Golfers carry at least seven kinds of clubs to help them make the best shots. The end of the club, called the *head,* can be made of wood or metal. Golfers must plan which club to use for each shot.

The officials who run the golf course decide on how many strokes should be needed to play each hole. This number is called the *par.* The best golfers may not need that many strokes to complete each hole. They play "under par." In golf, the best score is the lowest score.

In the United States, professional men golfers usually belong to the Professional Golfers' Association of America—the *PGA.* Women professionals play for the Ladies Professional Golf Association—the *LPGA.* Both the PGA and the LPGA hold competitions called *tournaments* that offer large money prizes for the winners. Amateur golfers are sometimes allowed to compete with the professionals in tournaments called *opens.*

Golf was first played in Scotland hundreds of years ago. Walter Hagen and Bobby Jones were leading golf players of the 1920s. The best golfers of recent years have included Jack Nicklaus, Arnold Palmer, Lee Trevino, and Nancy Lopez.

Goodyear, Charles

Charles Goodyear became famous for discovering how to make rubber usable in both cold and hot weather. He was born in 1800. As a young man, he worked in his father's hardware business. He was soon interested in finding a way to improve natural rubber.

Natural rubber isn't very useful. It softens when it gets hot and cracks when it gets cold. Charles Goodyear worked for five years

Goodyear's vulcanized rubber is used to make tires, rainwear, and sports equipment.

to find a way to make rubber useful in any temperature. In 1839, he mixed sulfur with the rubber. By accident, he dropped some of the mixture on a hot stove. To his surprise, it did not melt, and it stayed useful at cold temperatures, too. Goodyear called the new material *vulcanized rubber,* after Vulcan, the Roman god of fire.

Goodyear formed companies to make rubber products, but they lost money. He died a poor man in 1860. About 40 years later, early automobile makers started using vulcanized rubber for car tires. Today, vulcanized rubber is used for tires on trucks, buses, airplanes, and farm machinery, too. It is also used in bathing suits, raincoats, boots, shoes, balls and other toys, and hundreds of other things. One large rubber company still bears Charles Goodyear's name.

See also **rubber.**

goose, *see* **water birds**

gorilla, *see* **ape**

government

All of us live together with other people in families and communities. If everyone in a group did just as he or she pleased, the result would be confusion and perhaps even violence. Government exists to keep this from happening. A group of people may agree freely to have a certain kind of government. In other cases, a government may be forced upon the people by a few who have power.

There are many kinds of governments. A wandering band of herders has a government, although it may be very simple—just a few rules handed down by people in the group. Religious groups and sports teams have rules that govern their members. Cities, states, and nations, too, have governments. This article will discuss the governments of nations, including the United States.

What Governments Do   One of the main responsibilities of a government is to maintain order. Governments pass laws that say what people can and cannot do. Police see that the laws are obeyed. They try to catch people who disobey laws. Governments have courts to decide whether an accused person did or did not do something wrong. If the court decides the person is guilty, it then decides on the punishment.

Another important task of government is to defend a nation against its enemies. Nations have armed services ready to fight if the nation is attacked. The armed services also try to restore order if people within the nation *revolt*—try to overthrow their government. If a revolution succeeds, a new government comes into power.

Most governments today have many other responsibilities. They help their citizens by giving money for medical care, and to people who are old or out of work. In the United States, these jobs are handled by Medicare, Medicaid, and the social security system.

A government usually works to improve its country's *economy*—how it produces and sells things. For example, the United States government built a huge network of highways to help move people and goods. All these services are paid for by *taxes*—money people pay to the government. Governments collect taxes on products people buy and on the salaries people earn.

Local governments (left) provide local police and courts to help keep the peace. Garbage collection and local sewer systems help keep a region clean and wholesome. State and federal governments (right) build highways, train armed forces for use in case of war, inspect food products, and provide many other services.

Kinds of Government There are two main kinds of government. Under one kind of government, one person or a small group of people have most of the power. The rest of the people are allowed very little freedom. Today, government by one or a few is called a *dictatorship*. Many communist countries, like Cuba, are dictatorships. But they also exist in other countries. (*See* **monarchy** and **dictator**.)

Under the other main kind of government, the people hold most of the power. This is called a *democracy,* and it began in ancient Greece. In a democracy, the people make major decisions, usually by voting. They can write, speak, and meet together freely.

There are various kinds of democratic governments today. Britain, for example, has a queen, but she holds little power. The British elect representatives to a group called Parliament, which makes the laws.

The government of the United States is a democracy. Power is divided among three branches of government. The *executive* branch consists of the president, who proposes laws, and the president's advisers. The *legislative* branch, which makes laws, is the Congress. The third branch is the *judiciary* —the Supreme Court and other law courts. The judiciary explains the laws.

None of these branches can act alone. For example, Congress can pass a law. But it does not take effect unless the president signs it. Even if it is signed, the courts can later decide that it is unfair and should not be a law. This is called a system of *checks and balances.*

In the United States, power is divided between the national government and the state governments. This is called a *federal* system. Some powers, such as the right to declare war, belong only to the national government. Other powers, such as setting up school systems, belong only to the states.

See also **Constitution of the United States; democracy; Congress, United States; Supreme Court, United States; state government;** and **communism.**

Martha Graham introduced a new dance style called *modern dance.*

Graham, Martha

Martha Graham was an American dancer, dance teacher, and choreographer. She is famous for her dance style, called *modern dance.*

Graham was born near Pittsburgh, Pennsylvania, in 1893. She entered the Denishawn School of Dance in 1916 and studied with two great teachers. But she was not happy with what she learned. She felt that ballet dancers were too controlled and "pretty." She wanted to use dance to express the strong inner feelings all people have.

Graham began her own dance company in New York City in 1926. She based her style of dance on strong muscle movements that expressed emotions, such as fear, hate, joy, and love. Many of her dances were not graceful like ballet. At first, many people did not like them. They found the jerky movements shocking and ugly. But over the years, people came to like her dances more and more.

In all, Graham produced more than 170 works. One is *Appalachian Spring,* which she created with the American composer Aaron Copland. Her style influenced many dancers and teachers. Modern dance today owes much to Martha Graham.

grain

Grain is the seed from grasses. Some common grains are wheat, rice, corn, oats, barley, rye, sorghum, and millet.

Grains are among our most important foods. They have high amounts of carbohydrates, which are needed for energy. They also contain proteins, fats, and vitamins. Wheat, corn, and rye are ground into flour. The flour is then baked into bread, muffins, pancakes, and other foods. Barley, rice, millet, and corn are often steamed or boiled and eaten whole. Breakfast cereals and noodles are made of grains. Grains are also used to make alcoholic drinks.

Grains are important foods for animals, too. Farm animals eat corn and oats. They also eat *hay*—dried grain plants. Birds and mice eat the seeds of wild grasses.

Grains were among the first foods to be grown as crops. Wheat has been found in the remains of Stone Age camps and in the tombs of Egyptian pharaohs. Millet, too, dates back to the Stone Age.

Rye is the newest grain. It was first used in the days of ancient Rome. Rye does well even in poor growing conditions. Wheat grows best in good conditions. Some farmers grow wheat and rye together, so they will have plenty of grain no matter what happens. Rye and wheat flours can be mixed to make a light, tasty loaf of bread.

Most ancient civilizations relied on a single kind of grain. Wheat was the main crop of the ancient Babylonian, Egyptian, Greek, and Roman empires. The Inca, Aztec, and Maya grew corn. People stored large amounts of dry grain in order to have enough to eat when other foods were scarce. Grain was so important that ancient people prayed to grain gods and goddesses.

In the United States today, people use more wheat than any other kind of grain. We also eat corn, oats, and barley, but much of our corn, oats, and barley is fed to animals. In Latin America, corn and rice are still the most popular grains. People in the Soviet

Grains provide food for people around the world. In North America, wheat is made into cereals and many kinds of bread.

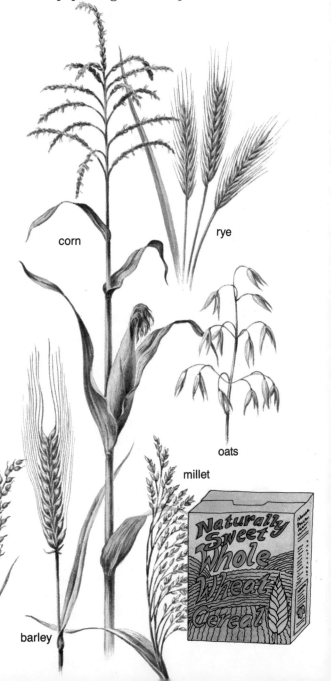

corn

rye

oats

millet

wheat

rice

barley

Vacuum pipes can suck wheat from the pile at left into the grain elevators at right. Grain from the elevators can be loaded automatically into railcars.

Union and Eastern Europe rely on rye. In parts of Africa and Asia, rice, sorghum, and millet are the important grains.

See also **grasses; bread; flour;** and **food.**

grain elevator

In many farming communities, the tallest building in sight is a grain elevator. *Grain* is a general name for the grass seeds we eat, such as wheat, corn, and rice. A grain elevator is a building or group of buildings that has special machines for loading, storing, and unloading grains. (*See* **grain.**)

Grain elevators are usually built near markets, at railroad crossings, in seaports, and in mills where flour is made. Grain from many farms is stored in the grain elevator. Later, the grain is moved onto railroad cars, boats, or trucks, which take it to other parts of the country.

Grain elevators are usually made of strong concrete. They must be able to hold many tons of grain. A large grain elevator may store over 10 million bushels of grain and stand as tall as 100 feet (30 meters).

Grain elevators often have several parts that handle different jobs. At the ground level, there is space for trucks or railroad cars to load and unload grain. Higher up are chutes and conveyor belts that carry the grain from one part of the grain elevator to another. There are also machines that blow the grain into storage bins.

See also **farming.**

Grand Canyon

The Grand Canyon, in northwestern Arizona, is a natural wonder famous the world over. It is a long, deep river valley with steep sides of rock. It is more than 200 miles (320 kilometers) long and up to 18 miles (29 kilometers) wide. At one point, it is more than 1 mile (1.6 kilometers) deep.

The Colorado River formed the Grand Canyon. Water from the river carried sand and silt, which *eroded*—wore away—soft rock in the riverbed. The water kept cutting deeper into the rock, and created the canyon's walls. This process took millions of years and is still continuing today.

The river's waters cut through and exposed layers of limestone, sandstone, granite, shale, and other kinds of rock. Each layer is a different color. Some are pink and violet. Others are brown and green, or gray and black. The colors seem to change constantly as the sun makes its way across the sky.

Each layer has a story to tell about Earth's history. Scientists have found *fossils*—remains—of many kinds of plants and animals that once lived in the canyon. Some are millions of years old.

American Indians lived in the Grand Canyon more than 4,000 years ago. The area was given its name by John Wesley Powell, who explored the canyon in 1869. Powell was a *geologist*—a scientist who studies the Earth. In his writings, Powell described the breathtaking views and natural beauty of the canyon. Today, over 2 million people travel to the Grand Canyon each year to see the sights first described by Powell.

Grand Canyon National Park was set up in 1919. It includes the Grand Canyon and the surrounding hills and rock formations. The park covers an area almost as large as the state of Delaware.

There are many roads and trails through the park. Many people go to the Grand Canyon to ride rafts or boats down the Colorado River. Mountain lions, deer, and bighorn sheep are familiar sights in the park, where hunting is not allowed. The park is also known for its large number of small, wild donkeys, called *burros.* Visitors to the park also enjoy horseback riding, fishing, and camping.

See also **canyon.**

The Colorado River carved out Arizona's amazing Grand Canyon over millions of years. The layers of rock on the canyon walls tell much about the history of the earth.

granite

Granite is one of the most common kinds of *igneous* rocks. Igneous rocks form when melted rock hardens.

The melted rock that forms granite comes from places deep within the earth where it is hot enough to melt rock. Melted rock moves more easily than the hot, unmelted rock around it. Gases in the melted rock force it upward, toward the cool surface.

As the rock rises, it cools, and crystals begin to form. One of these crystals is quartz. Others are feldspar and mica. As a result, granite is a light-colored rock made up of interlocking clumps or grains of gray and white quartz and pink or cream-colored feldspar. Stuck between the two minerals are shiny flakes of mica.

Granite is common in many mountain ranges. In the United States, you can see entire mountains of granite in Yosemite Park, California, and at Stone Mountain, Georgia, near Atlanta. Because it is hard and can be polished to a shiny surface, granite is used for buildings and monuments.

See also **crystal; Earth; mineral;** and **rock.**

Grant, Ulysses S.

Ulysses Simpson Grant was the 18th president of the United States. He served two terms, one after the other, from 1869 to 1877. Before that, he had become famous as the commander of the Union armies during the Civil War.

Grant was born in Point Pleasant, Ohio, in 1822. As a boy, he liked to work with horses and other animals on his family's farm. Grant's father, however, wanted his son to become a soldier. He asked their congressman to help Ulysses be chosen to go to the United States Military Academy at West Point, New York. Grant was admitted to West Point in 1839.

Grant had no interest in being a soldier. An average student, he graduated from West Point in 1843. He was a second lieutenant in

Grant led Union armies in the Civil War. He later became president of the U.S.

the Army when the Mexican-American War began in 1846. Grant fought bravely in many battles during the war. This experience helped him later, during the Civil War.

Grant married after the Mexican-American War. He left his wife and son behind when the Army transferred him out West, because he could not support them on his pay. Depressed and lonely, Grant resigned from the Army in 1854 and returned to his family. He failed as a farmer and a real estate salesman. He finally took a job in a leather goods store owned by his brothers.

The Union Army badly needed trained officers when the Civil War began in 1861. Grant rejoined the Army. He was first made a colonel, and then a general. In 1863, Grant's forces captured Vicksburg, Mississippi. In 1864, President Lincoln appointed Grant commander of the entire Union Army. Grant and his soldiers battled the Confederate forces of General Robert E. Lee. Lee was forced to surrender in 1865.

Grant became a famous war hero. This helped him win two Presidential elections. Historians agree that Grant was a poor president. He was not experienced in politics and he did not exert strong leadership. Though Grant himself was an honest man, many of the officials who served under him were not. But he remained popular until his death in 1885.

See also **Mexican War** and **Civil War.**

grape

A grape is a small, juicy berry. Grapes can be eaten fresh or made into jams, jellies, and juices. They can be dried to make raisins. In some parts of the world, most grapes are made into wine, a drink that contains alcohol. Grapes for eating fresh are often called *table grapes.*

Grapes grow wild in bunches on woody vines. Thousands of years ago, when people first learned to farm, they learned to grow grapes. Grapes grow best where summers are warm and dry and winters are cool.

In winter, the bare plants look dead. But in spring, they send up new shoots. Growers provide wire fences for the vines to climb on. The fences help the plant get enough sun and keep the fruit off the damp ground.

Grapes need an entire summer to ripen. In late summer, they are harvested, usually by hand. Growers *prune*—cut back—the grapevines in winter and in summer. This helps them control each plant's growth and the amount of grapes it produces.

Grape growers have learned to breed many delicious kinds of grapes. They can make new grape varieties by taking a cutting from one grape plant and *grafting* it onto the roots of another plant. For example, one grape variety may produce good grapes but get many kinds of plant diseases. When this variety is grafted onto the root of a variety that does not get many diseases, the result may be a plant that grows good grapes and is healthy. (*See* **fruit** and **plant breeding.**)

Making wine from grapes began in Europe. When Europeans came to the Americas, they brought their grapevines with them. Now wine grapes are grown in many parts of North and South America. In the United States, California is the major grape-growing state.

Early settlers found a few kinds of grapes growing wild in North America. The most familiar is the Concord grape, a member of the fox grape family. Concords have dark purple skins, light-colored insides, and a tart but pleasing flavor. They are often made into jelly, jam, and juice.

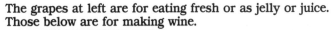

The grapes at left are for eating fresh or as jelly or juice. Those below are for making wine.

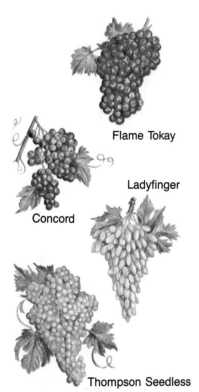

Flame Tokay

Ladyfinger

Concord

Thompson Seedless

graph

A graph is a picture that shows numbers or amounts. A graph is easier to understand than a list of numbers. Graphs let you compare two or more numbers or amounts to see how they are related.

A *pictograph* uses small figures or pictures. Each picture stands for a certain number—of people, cows, roses, dollars, or whatever the graph is about. The number of pictures or figures shows how many there are at a certain time or place.

Pictograph
Animals in Neighborhood

Dogs

Cats

Gerbils

If you color over the rows of pictures in a pictograph, you get a *bar graph.* Each bar stands for an amount. Like a pictograph, a bar graph helps you compare. Some bar graphs have vertical bars, while others have horizontal bars.

Let's say you want to make a bar graph about animals in your neighborhood. You will need to write the names of the kinds of animals across the bottom of your paper. On the side, starting at the bottom, write numbers that will show how many. Then, above each animal name, draw a bar as high as the number in your neighborhood. The height of the bars makes it easy to compare how many there are of each kind of animal.

Bar Graph
Animals in Neighborhood

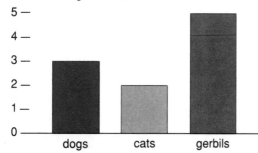

Line Graph
Animals in Neighborhood

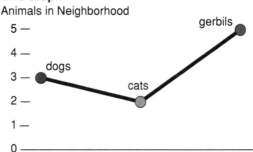

A *line graph* can be made from a bar graph by drawing lines that connect the tops of the bars. A line graph can also be drawn directly. If you wanted to show the numbers of neighborhood animals with a line graph, you would write the kinds of animals and the numbers as you did for the bar graph. Now put a dot at the correct number above each animal. Then connect the dots with lines.

Circle Graph
Animals in Neighborhood

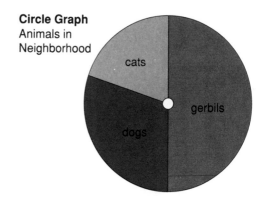

A *circle graph* lets you compare a whole amount and parts of that amount. For example, the circle could stand for your allowance. Each section of the circle shows a part of your allowance. If one-quarter of your allowance goes to buy lunch at school, you would label one-quarter of the circle "lunch money." A circle graph is sometimes called a *pie chart,* because it looks like a pie cut into pieces.

Graphs are used in newspapers, in reports, and on television. Schools, businesses, governments, and sports teams use graphs to show number information in a clear way.

grasses

Grasses are plants that have very tiny flowers. There are more grass plants than any other kind of plant in the world.

Many animals depend on grasses for food. Sheep, cattle, bison, zebras, antelopes, and other grazing animals feed mostly on grasses. Mice and rabbits are grass-eaters. Many insects use grasses for food, too. The giant pandas of China eat only one food—bamboo, which is a kind of grass.

Humans, too, eat grasses. Wheat, rye, corn, rice, and oats are all grasses. You eat the seeds of these grasses—*grains*. Breakfast cereals are made from grains. The grains are flaked, fluffed, popped, and prepared in other ways to produce different kinds of cereals. Often, grains are ground up to make flour. The flour is mixed with other ingredients and then cooked to make bread, spaghetti, and other foods. When you pop popcorn, you are cooking the seeds of corn. Although you may not think of corn as a kind of grass, it is. (*See* grain.)

Grasses are an important food for humans because their grain is very nutritious. If grain is dried and stored carefully, it will keep for a long time. (*See* corn; rice; and wheat.)

Many people plant grassy areas called *lawns* around homes. Grasses used for lawns must be tough to survive people walking and running on the lawn. Most grasses have upright stems. But many of the grasses we use for lawns have creeping stems that grow underground or just along the surface of the ground. The "blades" of grass we see are actually the leaves of the grass plant.

The largest plant in the grass family is bamboo, which grows taller than many trees.

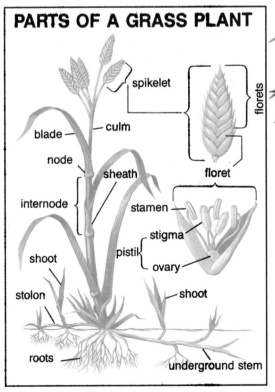

PARTS OF A GRASS PLANT

Grasses in lawns serve many purposes. They beautify homes with a bright green setting that is much prettier than bare soil. They give off water vapor, which helps keep homes comfortable on hot days. They also protect the soil by preventing *erosion*—the wearing away of the soil by water or wind. (*See* **erosion.**)

You may have looked at the flowers of grasses and not known they were flowers. Usually, grass flowers are very small and drab. They do not have petals. Some flowers need bright petals to attract the insects that pollinate them. But grass flowers are pollinated by the wind. (*See* **flower** and **flowering plant.**)

When grass flowers bloom, they produce large amounts of pollen. The tiny pollen grains are picked up and carried by any breeze. Allergy attacks can be caused by grass pollen. These attacks are sometimes called "hay fever," because they are most common when hay grasses are in bloom.

See also **grassland** and **plant.**

grasshopper

The grasshopper is an insect that jumps. It has very large, powerful back legs. A grasshopper can leap almost 90 centimeters (3 feet) into the air. That is like a human jumping one-third the length of a football field!

Most grasshoppers have two pairs of wings and can use them to fly. Grasshoppers

You can recognize a grasshopper by its long "jumping" legs.

can make sounds by rubbing their legs against their front wings. Some rub their back legs against their bodies. Sounds may be made to attract a mate, or to warn of approaching enemies.

A grasshopper has no ears. It hears through structures on its body called *tympana.* The tympana look like tightly stretched drumskins. They are very sensitive to sound. Grasshoppers can hear sounds too high-pitched for humans to hear. All grasshoppers have five eyes. Two are *compound* eyes with thousands of lenses. Each lens sees a small piece of the whole "picture."

Grasshoppers are plant-eaters. Their mouthparts are designed to bite off and chew leaves and tender stems. Some grasshoppers are serious pests because they eat crops. Grasshoppers called *locusts* may form huge groups—*swarms*—containing millions or even billions of locusts. When the swarm is migrating to new breeding grounds, the locusts eat everything in their path.

grassland

If you drive through Kansas and eastern Colorado, you will cross a vast sea of grasses. In eastern Kansas the land is hilly. But as you go west, it becomes flat. You can see for miles in all directions. The only trees in sight are growing along the banks of rivers. The rest is a grassland—the North American prairie.

What Causes Grasslands Grasslands have *droughts*—long periods without rain or snow. Grasses can survive droughts. The leaves aboveground dry up and die, but the roots filled with stored food survive. When the rains finally come, the grasses begin growing again and soon cover the area with green.

Grasses survive well during a drought, but few trees can. For this reason, there are few trees in grasslands. The trees in the North American prairie are mostly along rivers. When there is no rain, the trees can still get water from the rivers.

This wild grassland is in Wind Cave National Park, South Dakota. Most grassland in North America is now farmland, producing wheat, corn, and many other crops.

The main plants in grasslands are *perennial* grasses. Their roots live for many years. Each year they send up new leaves. Many of the grassland animals are pale in color. Their fur, feathers, or scales are light brown or gray. These colors help them blend with the soil and the dried grasses.

Grass and Fire Fires help grasslands remain healthy. During times of drought, the dead grasses pile up faster than they can decay. If too much dead grass piles up, it is difficult for healthy new grass to grow. But this does not usually happen. Sometimes, lightning strikes the dried grass and causes a fire. Other times, the dead grass just bursts into flame.

To understand this, it helps to know how decay works. When bacteria and fungi decay dead grass, heat builds up in the decaying material. When there is enough heat, a fire starts.

Before Europeans settled the North American prairie, Indians had learned about the importance of fire to healthy grass. They regularly set fire to large parts of the prairie to improve the grass for their horses and for the animals the Indians used for food.

No matter how the fire starts, the results are like someone clearing up the area. The dead grasses are burned up. With the next rain, new grasses begin growing in a clear environment.

Fire is another reason why there are so few trees in grasslands. Only a few trees, such as the burr oak, can survive a grass fire when they are young. In some parts of the Eastern prairie, the grassland is interrupted every few miles by a small group of fire-resistant burr oaks.

Grasslands occur in many areas of the world. The grasslands of eastern Europe and the Soviet Union are called *steppes.* African grasslands are the *veldt* and South American grasslands are *pampas.* Each of these grasslands has characteristics similar to the North American prairie.

The North American Prairie In North America, the prairie extends from the broadleaf forest in the east to the Rocky Mountains in the west. This grassland receives 30 to 150 centimeters (12 to 60 inches) of rain and snow each year. The western part of the prairie is drier than the eastern part. (*See* **Great Plains.**)

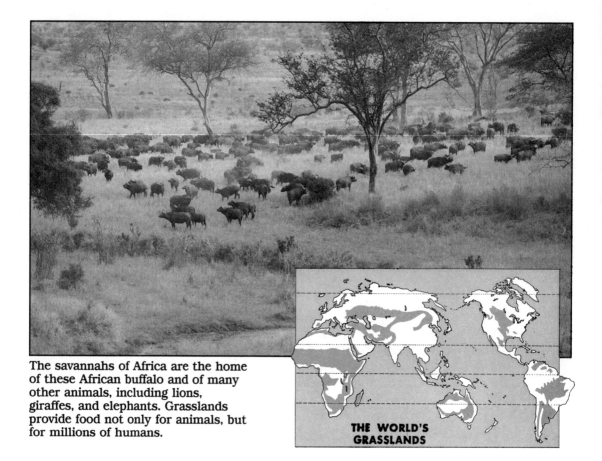

The savannahs of Africa are the home of these African buffalo and of many other animals, including lions, giraffes, and elephants. Grasslands provide food not only for animals, but for millions of humans.

THE WORLD'S GRASSLANDS

Most grasslands have many grazing animals, but there are only a few in North America. About 150 years ago, thousands of large, furry bison roamed through the prairie. But today these animals are no longer wild. They live in National Parks or on farms. The prong-horned antelope lives in the northern part of this grassland. In winter, elk and mule deer may come down from the Rocky Mountains to feed on the prairie, but they are not a common sight.

Foxes, coyotes, owls, and hawks prey on the mice and rabbits. Many kinds of snakes, including rattlesnakes, live here, too. Some toads and lizards also make their homes in the prairie.

Savannahs A savannah is a special kind of tropical grassland. Savannahs are found between deserts and broadleaf forests in South America, Africa, Asia, and Australia. These grasslands also have trees growing in them. The trees grow far apart. They remind one of shade trees spaced on a lawn.

Only certain trees can grow in a savannah, because trees there must be able to survive periods of drought. Most of them lose their leaves when dry weather comes, even though the temperatures are not cold. Trees in savannahs often have large, sharp thorns. The thorns may keep animals from eating the tree's leaves. In Africa, acacia trees are common in savannahs. In Australia, the common trees are eucalyptus.

A savannah is home for many animals. In Africa, there are antelopes, elephants, zebras, and giraffes living on the savannah. The Australian savannah is the home of kangaroos and koalas.

Fires are just as important to savannahs as to pure grasslands. Fires in savannahs kill small trees and prevent the area from becoming a forest.

Farming the Grasslands For centuries, grasslands have been used for grazing cattle and sheep.

When Europeans first saw the North American prairie, they thought crops could not grow there. They were wrong. Grasslands have deep, rich soil. At first, farmers had trouble plowing the tough grass. Soon, new plows were developed that worked better in the prairie. Farmers turned under the prairie grasses and planted wheat, corn, and other crops. Since wheat and corn are grasses, it is not surprising that they grow well in fertile grasslands.

Today, the world's grasslands are major sources of food. In North America, the prairie is so important for farming that it is called the "nation's breadbasket."

But there has been a price. Very little of the original prairie is left. Some patches are preserved in parks, and can be visited. Spring, when the prairie is in flower, is the best time to visit them.

See also **prairie.**

gravity

If you have ever thrown a ball, you know that the old saying "What goes up must come down" is true. What makes it true is gravity. Gravity is the force that we feel on the surface of the earth as weight.

You and the earth are very close together. The earth pulls on you and you pull on the earth. This attraction—pulling on one another—is called a *gravitational force*. This force exists because you and the earth have mass. *Mass* is a measure of how much matter is in something. It is measured in such units as kilograms and grams. How strong this force is depends on how close two bodies are and how great their masses are. Since the earth is many, many times your mass, you feel the earth pulling on you. This force keeps you on the ground instead of floating up in the air.

Gravity on the earth's surface acts the same way with all objects. It makes everything fall at the same rate. When a glass falls down from a table to the floor, it is moving from one place to another place closer to the center of the earth.

On the moon, the pull of gravity is much less than it is on the earth. That is because the moon has a much smaller mass than does the earth. If you weigh 60 pounds (132 kilograms) on Earth, you would weigh only 10 pounds (22 kilograms) on the moon. But you would weigh about 158½ pounds (348.5 kilograms) on Jupiter, the planet with the greatest mass.

Gravity affects everything in the universe. There is a gravitational force between the sun and the planets and between the earth and the moon. The sun is much larger than the planets, so they are held in their path around the sun by this attraction. The gravitational force of the earth keeps the moon circling around it.

The theory of gravity was first proposed by Sir Isaac Newton. According to Newton, he got the idea when he saw an apple fall from a tree. He saw the apple fall and thought that the same force must cause the moon to move in its path around the earth. Since Newton's time, gravity has been studied by many scientists, including Albert Einstein.

See also **Newton, Sir Isaac** and **Einstein, Albert.**

Gravity attracts—pulls—objects to the earth's surface.

Great Britain, *see* United Kingdom

Great Lakes

The Great Lakes form the largest body of fresh water in the world. The five connected lakes lie in east-central North America. They are named Huron, Ontario, Michigan, Erie, and Superior. The first letter of each lake's name can be put together with the others to spell the word *homes.* Many people think of this word to help them remember the names of the Great Lakes.

Lake Michigan is the only one of the Great Lakes that lies completely in the United States. Lakes Superior, Huron, Erie, and Ontario form part of the border between the United States and Canada. The Great Lakes are joined to each other by canals, rivers, and *straits*—narrow waterways that connect two larger bodies of water. Ships travel from the Great Lakes east to the Atlantic Ocean or south to the Gulf of Mexico. Important ports on the Great Lakes include Chicago, Illinois; Milwaukee, Wisconsin; Detroit, Michigan;

Cleveland, Ohio; Buffalo, New York; and Toronto, Ontario.

History The Great Lakes were formed thousands of years ago, during the last ice age. A giant glacier inching over the land dug out five huge, deep holes. When the glacier melted, its water filled the holes, creating the Great Lakes. (*See* **ice age** and **glacier.**)

The Ottawa, Huron, Erie, Iroquois, and Kickapoo were among the Indians who lived near the Great Lakes for hundreds of years. In the 1600s, French explorers began to build forts and trading posts along the lakes. During the War of 1812, the United States and Great Britain fought naval battles on Lakes Erie and Ontario.

The Great Lakes played an important role in the growth of the United States. Lumber, coal, and iron ore were some of the raw materials shipped to different parts of the country from ports located on the Great Lakes.

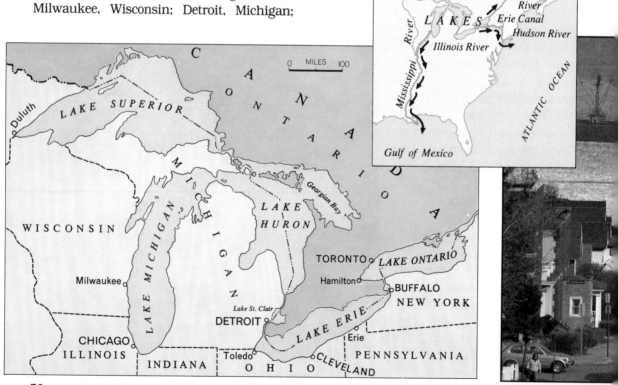

Ways to the Sea Lake Ontario is the farthest east of the Great Lakes. It empties into the St. Lawrence River, which flows into the Atlantic Ocean. The canals and dams of the St. Lawrence Seaway allow ships to sail the entire length of the St. Lawrence River. So ships can travel from Duluth, Minnesota, the westernmost port of the Great Lakes, all the way to the Atlantic. This is a distance of almost 2,500 miles (4,025 kilometers). The Great Lakes and St. Lawrence Seaway form one of the most important inland waterways in the world.

Smaller ships can reach the Atlantic in two other ways. They can sail from Lake Michigan through the Illinois Waterway into the Mississippi River. From there, they travel south to the Gulf of Mexico. Ships can also sail from Lake Erie into New York State's Erie Canal, which takes them east to the Hudson River. Then they sail south on the Hudson to the Atlantic Ocean.

Giant ore ships (below) carry iron ore from mines near Lake Superior to steel mills near Lake Michigan and Lake Erie. The map at left shows that ships can travel from the Great Lakes to the Mississippi River or the Atlantic Ocean.

The Lakes Lake Superior, the largest freshwater lake in the world, covers 31,700 square miles (82,103 square kilometers). At its deepest, Lake Superior is 1,333 feet (406 meters) deep. Early French explorers called it *Lac Supérieur,* which means "upper lake." Superior is the farthest west of the Great Lakes. It empties into Lake Huron through the Saint Mary's River and the Sault Sainte Marie Canals.

Lake Michigan takes its name from the Indian word *michigami,* which means "big water." It is the third-largest Great Lake, covering 22,300 square miles (57,757 square kilometers). Lake Michigan flows into Lake Huron through the Straits of Mackinac.

Lake Huron, the second-largest Great Lake, covers an area of 23,050 square miles (59,699 square kilometers). It empties into Lake Erie to the south.

Lake Erie is the second-smallest of the Great Lakes. It covers 9,910 square miles (25,667 square kilometers). The Welland Canal connects Lake Erie to Lake Ontario. The Niagara River also joins the two lakes. The waters of this river form the world-famous Niagara Falls.

Lake Ontario is the smallest of the Great Lakes. Its name comes from an Indian word that means "land of beautiful waters." Lake Ontario covers 7,550 square miles (19,555 square kilometers).

The Great Lakes are used for fishing and recreation. But in recent years, the lakes have been polluted by industrial and other wastes. The United States and Canada are both working to solve this problem.

Great Plains

The Great Plains are vast, dry grasslands in west-central North America. Large herds of buffalo roamed the Plains more than a century ago. They were hunted by Crow, Sioux, Comanche, Cheyenne, and other Plains Indians, who lived there.

Today, the Great Plains are among the least-populated areas of the United States.

Wind on the western Great Plains blows tumbleweeds across huge open stretches.

Most of the land is flat and treeless. Trees grow only along the banks of rivers and streams. Large sheep and cattle ranches, wheat farms, and mines are scattered across the grasslands. The area's only large city is Denver, Colorado. Denver sits at the western edge of the Plains, where they meet the Rocky Mountains.

The Great Plains extends about 400 miles (640 kilometers) east from the foothills of the Rocky Mountains. From their northern boundary in Canada to their southern end in Texas, the Plains stretch for 2,500 miles (4,020 kilometers).

The area covered by the Great Plains includes the eastern parts of Montana, Wyoming, Colorado, and New Mexico, and the western parts of North and South Dakota, Nebraska, Kansas, Oklahoma, and Texas. The Great Plains also include southern Alberta and Saskatchewan, two of Canada's three Prairie Provinces.

The *climate* of the Great Plains—their yearly pattern of weather—has always discouraged people from living there. Many pioneers traveled across the Great Plains during the late 1800s, but few stayed. The climate was too dry for farming. There was not enough wood to build houses and fences. The area is hot in the summer and very cold in the winter. The winds are often strong and harsh, and there are many blizzards during the winter months.

Many rivers, including the Missouri, Yellowstone, Platte, and Arkansas, begin in the Rockies and flow across the Plains. These rivers often flood in the spring, when the snow melts in the Rocky Mountains. But there is so little rain during the summer that many rivers dry up or become small, trickling streams.

The eastern part of the Great Plains receives more rainfall than the western part. So most of the wheat farms are located in the eastern section. The dry western Great Plains have good pasturelands for sheep and cattle. Oil, gold, iron ore, and coal are found in many Plains areas.

Great Salt Lake

Great Salt Lake, in the northwestern corner of Utah, is the largest saltwater lake in the

Western Hemisphere. Normally, the lake covers about 1,700 square miles (4,403 square kilometers). The lake grows when rains are heavy. In most places, it is less than 15 feet (4.6 meters) deep. But its waters are about six times as salty as ocean water.

About 10,000 years ago, Great Salt Lake was part of a huge body of water that geologists call Lake Bonneville. As temperatures rose, Lake Bonneville gradually dried up, creating Great Salt Lake and several smaller lakes.

Freshwater rivers flow into Great Salt Lake, but no water flows out. Instead, the waters of the lake *evaporate*—dry up— leaving salt behind. Mineral and chemical companies remove some to make table salt.

Great Salt Lake is too salty for fish and most other forms of life. But the lake contains brine shrimp, some tiny flies, and blue-green algae. Herons, terns, and seagulls are among the birds that nest on small islands in Great Salt Lake.

The large amount of salt in the lake makes its waters very heavy and dense. It is almost impossible to sink in Great Salt Lake. People have fun floating and bobbing around like corks in its waters.

Great Wall of China

Imagine a wall that stretches all the way from Washington, D.C., to Denver, Colorado. That distance, 1,500 miles (2,400 kilometers) is the length of the Great Wall of China, the longest structure in the world.

In the 400s B.C., China's rulers decided that a wall was needed to keep out invaders from the North. The Chinese began building the Great Wall and worked on it off and on for 2,000 years. Many men died from the hard labor.

The average height of the wall is 25 feet (7.6 meters)—the same measurement as the thickness of the base. The wall narrows at the top to about 15 feet (4.6 meters). The top was used as a roadway. There were once as many as 40,000 watchtowers along the wall.

Packed earth forms the core of the Great Wall. In most places, the wall is covered with brick or stone. Altogether, there is enough material in the Great Wall to build a wall 6 feet (2 meters) high around the earth at its middle—the equator.

In spite of its size, invaders were able to break through the Great Wall. Tourists come to China to see the parts that still stand.

The Great Wall was built to protect China from invaders from central Asia. Building it was one of the biggest projects in world history.

Greece

Capital: Athens
Area: 50,944 square miles (131,944 square kilometers)
Population (1985): about 10,000,000
Official language: Greek

Greece is a small country in the southeastern corner of Europe. It is about the size of the state of Alabama. Greece was very important in the ancient world, more than 2,500 years ago. It is no longer so powerful, but it is still a crossroads between Europe and the countries of the Middle East. The Greek people are proud of their past and of their culture today.

Land Mainland Greece is a peninsula. It looks like a bear claw reaching into the Mediterranean Sea to the south. Just off the mainland, Greece has more than 2,000 islands. People live on about 200 of them.

Most of Greece is rugged and mountainous. The Pindus Mountains run from north to south through the peninsula. Greece's northern borders with Albania and Yugoslavia are also mountainous.

One of the flatter parts of Greece is the Plain of Thessaly, near the center of the peninsula. Even here, mountains loom in the background. At the edge of the Plain is Mount Olympus, Greece's highest and most famous mountain. Its snowcapped peak can be seen from miles away. The ancient Greeks believed that their gods lived on the slopes of Mount Olympus. (*See* **gods and goddesses.**)

Greece's winters are mild and wet. Summers are hot and dry. Most of the land is rocky and dry. Only about a quarter of it is suitable for farming. Farmers depend on crops that grow without much water, such as wheat, olives, and some fruit. Sheep graze on grasses that grow on the mountainsides.

Lamb is an important food for the Greeks.

Fish, too, is an important food. Greece has 9,000 miles of ocean shoreline, and fishing is one of its main industries. Fishing boats and drying fishing nets are a common sight.

History The ancient Greek states were strong and independent until the 300s B.C. (*See* **Greece, ancient.**)

After that, Greek lands became part of many other great empires. Around 150 B.C., Greece became a part of the spreading Roman Empire. The Romans adopted many Greek ideas. Roman gods were modeled after the ancient Greek gods, and many Roman buildings imitated Greek buildings.

After A.D. 300, the Roman Empire divided in two. Greece became part of the eastern part of the old Roman Empire. This was called the Byzantine Empire. Its capital was Constantinople, which was founded by the Roman emperor Constantine the Great. Constantinople (today called Istanbul) became an important city to early Christians. The Greek Orthodox Church grew out of the Christian traditions of Constantinople. (*See* **Constantine the Great.**)

Greece remained part of the Byzantine Empire for more than 1,000 years. In the 1400s, Ottoman rulers from Turkey conquered the Byzantine Empire. For the next 300 years, Greece was part of the Ottoman Empire.

In the 1700s, Greek patriots began to seek independence. Finally in the 1830s, after many years of war, Greece became free. Since the 1920s, Greece has seen many political changes—many different governments and leaders.

People Greece is not a wealthy nation. Most Greeks are poor. One reason for the many changes of government is that poor people hope a new government may bring a better economy.

Almost one-third of the Greek people live in the capital city of Athens. Greeks in the countryside and on the islands live very simply. Many have no electricity and no running water. Most are farmers or fisherman.

ELEVATION
Feet
5000 — 10000
2000 — 5000
1000 — 2000
0 — 1000

MILES
100

Greeks today speak modern Greek. It grew from the ancient Greek language and uses the same alphabet, developed more than 3,000 years ago.

Most Greeks are members of the Greek Orthodox Church. Its traditions and rituals are similar to those of the Roman Catholic Church. Church leaders play a leading role in the country's life.

Tourism is an important Greek industry. People come from all over the world to visit the bustling city of Athens and the beautiful Greek islands. Visitors can view the ruins of ancient Greece while enjoying the pleasures of modern Greece. The Greek people are fun-loving and friendly. Tourists enjoy Greek food and lively Greek music and dancing. They buy Greek handcrafts—pottery, embroidery, and woven handbags and rugs.

This hillside town is on the Greek island of Karpathos, between Rhodes and Crete. People were living on these islands long before recorded history.

Greece, ancient

In ancient times, the people of Greece developed a way of life that still influences us today. The Greeks had the world's first democracy. They were the first people to recognize the importance of the individual. They felt that the human mind and spirit could achieve almost anything. Ancient Greek civilization reached its height in the 400s B.C.—about 2,500 years ago.

The main part of Greece is a rocky peninsula surrounded on three sides by water. The ancient Greeks settled along the coasts and plains in small, independent communities called *city-states*. The land was hard to farm. Not enough crops could be grown. So, many Greeks sailed to islands and other lands around the Mediterranean Sea. There they set up more city-states. In all, there were about 700 Greek city-states.

The most famous Greek city-state was Athens. Its people developed the world's first democracy. But not all Greek city-states were democracies. Some were ruled by strong kings, others by small groups of leaders. (*See* **Athens** and **democracy**.)

Everyday Life Most Greeks were farmers or traders. The most important people in a city-state were its *citizens*—men whose fathers had been born in Greece. Next, there were the free noncitizens—women, children, and people from other city-states. *Serfs* —poor noncitizens—could own land, but they were not allowed to leave the place where they were born. *Slaves* were the property of individual citizens.

The ancient Greeks lived simply. They ate mainly bread, cheese, olives, and fruit. Their clothing was plain, and they spent a great deal of time outdoors in the pleasant, mild climate. They loved sports, and often held contests. The Olympic Games started as contests held in the ancient Greek city-state of Olympia. (*See* **Olympic Games**.)

The Greeks worshiped many gods, and believed they were related. Zeus was the king of the gods. His wife, Hera, was the goddess of marriage and birth. Zeus's son Apollo was the god of light and poetry. Apollo's sister, Athena, was the goddess of wisdom. According to Greek legends, the gods often squabbled among themselves. But they usually were friendly toward humans and sometimes helped their favorites. Unlike other ancient peoples, the Greeks did not live in fear of angering their gods.

Literature and Art Two of the most famous pieces of ancient Greek literature are the *Iliad* and the *Odyssey*. These are long poems about the heroes of a long war between Greece and the ancient city of Troy. We think a blind poet named Homer composed both the *Iliad* and the *Odyssey*. (*See* **Homer**.)

This statue of a woman serves as a column of a temple on the Acropolis in Athens.

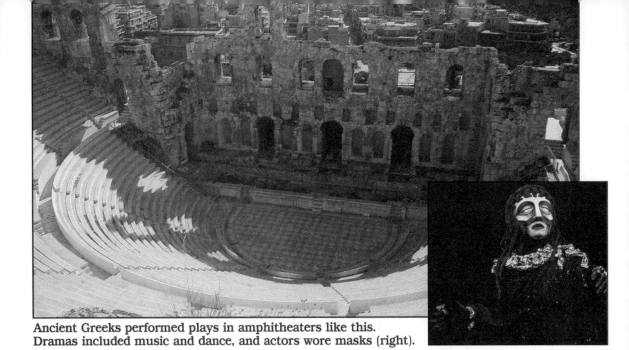

Ancient Greeks performed plays in amphitheaters like this. Dramas included music and dance, and actors wore masks (right).

The Greeks wrote *drama*—plays. Plays were usually performed in outdoor theaters. Some plays were *tragedies*—sad stories about gods and heroes. *Comedies* looked at the funny side of everyday life and ended happily. Ancient Greek literature influenced later writers all over the world. It is still read and studied today.

The Greeks developed a simple but noble style of building. Marble or limestone columns supported the roofs of their public buildings and their temples. Every city-state had at least one temple honoring a god or goddess. Each temple was built on a hill called an *acropolis* in the center of a city. The *Parthenon,* a temple that honors the goddess Athena, still stands in Athens. (*See* **Acropolis** and **architecture.**)

The magnificent sculptures of ancient Greece have been a model for artists ever since. These sculptures often show the beauty of the perfect human body. The marble carvings of humans and gods are so lifelike that they seem to move.

Greek Thought The Greeks wanted to find the answers to some basic questions. They asked, "How can one learn the truth?" "Which is the best kind of government?" "What is happiness?" Men who sought to answer these questions were called *philosophers.* They used reason—the power of the human mind to think through ideas and draw conclusions—to answer their many questions.

Socrates was an important Greek philosopher who encouraged people to examine their beliefs. One of his pupils, Plato, was interested in separating reality from things that only appear to be real. Plato's pupil, Aristotle, tried to gather together all human knowledge in order to understand the basic laws of the universe. (*See* **Socrates.**)

Greek thinkers made discoveries in geometry and science. Greek scientists believed the earth was round, and calculated the distance around it at the equator. One Greek scientist argued that the earth revolved around the sun, an idea that was not accepted until 2,000 years later. Another Greek thinker, Democritus, was the first to say that matter was made up of atoms. Archimedes, a mathematician, made important discoveries showing why a lever works and how volume could be measured. (*See* **atom** and **Archimedes.**)

In the 300s B.C., Greece was united with the civilization of Macedonia to the north. During this time, the Macedonian king, Alexander the Great, conquered a vast territory. Alexander admired the Greeks, and started cities like the cities of the Greeks everywhere he went. Greek culture was then spread throughout much of the civilized world. (*See* **Alexander the Great.**)

greenhouse

A greenhouse is a specially designed room or building used for growing plants. Light, temperature, and moisture can be controlled in a greenhouse. Perfect growing conditions for plants can be supplied no matter what the weather is outside. Greenhouses also allow people to grow plants that come from other parts of the world, or to grow warm-weather vegetables in winter.

A greenhouse is usually made of a metal or wooden frame covered with glass or clear plastic. The glass or plastic roof and sides allow sunlight to enter all day long. When the sunlight strikes solid objects inside the greenhouse, it warms them. The heat the objects give off is trapped inside, warming the air. This is called the *greenhouse effect.* Some gases in the atmosphere, such as carbon dioxide, can also trap heat this way. (*See* **carbon dioxide.**)

The first greenhouses were used in ancient Rome for growing cucumbers in the winter. Today's commercial greenhouses produce huge crops of tomatoes, cucumbers, lettuce, and flowers. People who are trying to conserve energy may use greenhouses attached to their houses as a source of heat.

A greenhouse lets in sunlight and traps its warmth.

Greenland

Greenland, the world's largest island, is located in the North Atlantic Ocean between Canada and Iceland. Most of Greenland lies above the Arctic Circle. Few people live there, because it is so cold and frozen. About 85 percent of the island is covered with ice over 1 mile (1.6 kilometers) deep. In fact, there is enough ice in Greenland to cover the entire United States east of the Mississippi River.

Greenland is often considered part of North America. But it is a province of Denmark, 1,300 miles (2,100 kilometers) across the Atlantic Ocean in northern Europe.

Greenland's coast is lined with mountains and *fiords*—long, narrow fingers of the sea. The *glacier*—ice sheet—that covers most of the island pushes ice out toward the coast. Sometimes, huge chunks of ice called *icebergs* break off. There are many small islands off the coast of Greenland. (*See* **glacier; fiord;** and **iceberg.**)

Almost all of Greenland's 55,000 people are of mixed Eskimo and Danish descent. Most live on or near the southwestern coast, which is the warmest part of the island. Godthaab, the capital and largest city, is located here.

Grass and some trees grow in southwestern Greenland, but most of the land is rocky. There are no railroads and very few roads. Most people travel from place to place by boat, plane, or dogsled.

Over one-third of the people in Greenland make their living by fishing. Others herd sheep and reindeer or work in mines. There are no large farms, but some people grow small amounts of food for themselves.

Eskimo from North America were probably the first people to live in Greenland. In the late 900s, Vikings from Scandinavia began a settlement on the southwest coast. This made Greenland the first European colony in the New World. The island was first called Greenland by the Viking leader Eric the Red. He hoped that the name would attract more settlers. (*See* **Vikings.**)

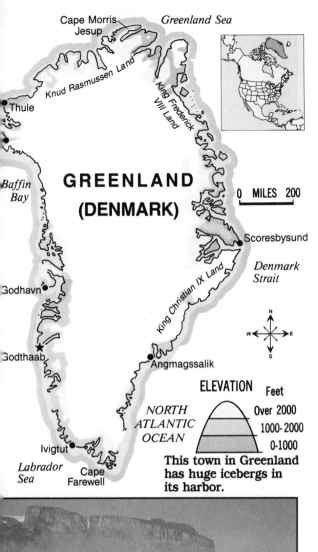

GREENLAND
(DENMARK)

Cape Morris Jesup
Greenland Sea
Knud Rasmussen Land
Thule
King Frederick VIII Land
Baffin Bay
Godhavn
Godthaab
Ivigtut
Labrador Sea
Cape Farewell
King Christian IX Land
Scoresbysund
Denmark Strait
Angmagssalik
NORTH ATLANTIC OCEAN

0 MILES 200

N
W E
S

ELEVATION   Feet
Over 2000
1000-2000
0-1000

This town in Greenland has huge icebergs in its harbor.

In 1261, the colony became part of Norway. Norway and Denmark were united in 1380. When they separated in the 1800s, Greenland became a Danish colony.

Since World War II, Greenland has been important to the defense of North America. The United States has military, radar, and weather bases in Greenland.

Grenada, *see* **West Indies**

Gretzky, Wayne

Wayne Gretzky is a professional ice hockey player. He is considered one of hockey's top athletes. Admiring fans often call him "the Great Gretzky." Gretzky was only 19 years old in 1980, when he won the Most Valuable Player Award of the National Hockey League (NHL). He was the youngest player ever to win the award. He has since won the award more times than any other player in the history of hockey—eight times as of the 1986-to-1987 season.

Gretzky was born in Brantford, Ontario, in 1961. He began playing hockey when he was 6 years old. When he was 17, Gretzky joined the Edmonton Oilers, a professional team. Some people thought he was too skinny to be a pro star. Others said he could not skate fast enough or shoot the puck hard enough.

Gretzky soon showed his critics how wrong they were. He won the Most Valuable Player award again and again. Gretzky scored 212 points for the Oilers during the 1981-to-1982 season. In hockey, a player gets a point for either a goal or an *assist*—a pass to another player who scores a goal. No NHL player had ever before scored over 200 points in a season. Gretzky's total broke the old NHL record of 164 points—which he had set himself a year earlier. He has since broken this record again, too.

See also **hockey.**

Wayne Gretzky drives toward the goal with the puck for the Edmonton Oilers.

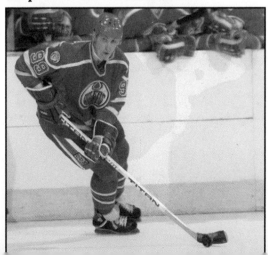

Grimm brothers

The Grimm brothers—Jacob and Wilhelm —lived in Germany in the 1800s. They are famous for their collection of folktales. The collection—called *Grimm's Fairy Tales*—includes such favorites as "Cinderella," "Snow White," "Hansel and Gretel," and "Little Red Riding Hood."

The Grimm brothers did not make up these stories. They traveled through Germany asking village people to tell stories they had heard from their parents or grandparents. Often, they heard the same story again and again, in different places. The Grimms realized that some of these tales had been told for hundreds or even thousands of years. No one knew where they first began.

The Grimm brothers decided to collect the stories and write them down so that none would be forgotten. Soon after the tales were published, they were translated into many other languages, including English.

The Grimm brothers were also interested in language and how it changes. They were two of the greatest language students of the 1800s. But most people still remember them best for the fairy tales they collected.

See also **fairy tale.**

groundhog

The groundhog—also called a *woodchuck* —is a member of the squirrel family. But the groundhog is about a foot long and too clumsy to climb trees. It digs a burrow in the ground. The burrow has several "rooms" and usually two or three entrances.

Groundhogs are found in fields and woods. Their favorite food is clover. Usually, they eat in the early morning and late afternoon. They spend the rest of the time lying in the sun or sleeping in their burrows.

In autumn, groundhogs prepare for winter by eating a lot and getting very fat. Then they go into their burrows and *hibernate* —go into a very deep sleep—until warmer weather returns. When they leave their burrows in spring, their weight is back to normal. Their bodies use up the extra fat while they sleep.

Some people celebrate February 2 as Groundhog Day. They believe that on this day the groundhogs come out to check the weather. According to legend, if the weather is cloudy and the groundhog does not see its shadow, spring will be early. If the day is sunny and the groundhog sees its shadow, cold weather will last six more weeks. But there is no proof that groundhogs are good weather forecasters!

Groundhogs make a network of underground tunnels to live in and store food in.

As people grow, their proportions change. A baby's head makes up about one-third of its body length. An adult's head makes up only about one-seventh of body length.

growth, human

A newborn baby usually weighs 6 to 9 pounds (2.5 to 4 kilograms) and is 19 to 21 inches (48 to 53 centimeters) long. Within half a year, the baby will weigh twice as much as at birth. Within two years, the child may weigh four times as much. By the time the child grows into an adult, he or she will probably weigh between 100 and 200 pounds. And he or she will probably be between 5 and 6 feet tall. This process is human growth.

Human growth begins before a baby is born. A sperm and an egg cell join together in the mother's body to form one single cell too small to see without a microscope. This cell divides many times to form a ball of several dozen cells. The ball of cells grows and develops into a human being inside the mother's body. During this time, the mother's bloodstream carries food and oxygen to the baby. After nine months of growth, the baby is ready to be born.

A human grows faster in the first two years than at any other time in his or her life. But humans continue to grow for many years after that. During childhood, boys and girls grow at about the same rate.

At about age 10 to 12, girls and boys again start to grow. This growth starts earlier in girls than it does in boys. Many girls around the age of 12 may be taller and weigh more than boys the same age. The growth spurt starts later for most boys than for girls. But once it starts, it lasts longer, and most boys grow more than most girls.

Some people grow larger than others. It is not unusual for a girl to grow taller and heavier than many boys her age. Many things help decide how tall and heavy a person becomes. Diet and exercise have something to do with it, but the most important thing is *heredity.* Children of large parents tend to grow large. Children of small parents tend to be small. Most differences in size are quite normal—human beings come in many sizes and shapes.

Sometimes, a child does not grow normally because he or she cannot make enough of the chemical called *human growth hormone.* Scientists have learned how to make human growth hormone. In some cases, doctors can give a child more of this hormone to help him or her grow to normal adult size.

By the end of the teen years, most humans have reached their full height. They never grow any taller. In fact, people may become slightly shorter as they age, because their joints compress. Grown-ups *can* grow in another way, however. They can gain weight.

Guam, *see* Pacific Islands

Guatemala, *see* Central America

Guinea, *see* Africa

Guinea-Bissau, *see* Africa

Gulf of Mexico

The Gulf of Mexico is the part of the Atlantic Ocean that borders the southeast coast of North America. The Gulf forms a basin that is almost completely surrounded by the United States, Mexico, and Cuba. It extends about 1,000 miles (1,609 kilometers) from east to west, and about 775 miles (1,247 kilometers) north to south.

The Gulf is connected to the Caribbean Sea by the Yucatán Channel, between Mexico's Yucatán Peninsula and the western tip of Cuba. The Straits of Florida, between the southern tip of Florida and northern Cuba, connect the Gulf of Mexico to the rest of the Atlantic Ocean.

Texas, Louisiana, Mississippi, Alabama, and Florida all border the Gulf of Mexico, and are known as the "Gulf States." The Gulf is a major sea route for goods entering and leaving North America. As a result, many cities along the Gulf of Mexico have become important ports. In the United States, these include the cities of Brownsville and Galveston, Texas; Mobile, Alabama; and Pensacola and Tampa, Florida. Other major Gulf ports are Vera Cruz, Mexico, and Havana, Cuba.

Several rivers flow into the Gulf of Mexico. The Mississippi River and the Rio Grande are the largest. The city of New Orleans, Louisiana, is located on the Mississippi River just north of where the river empties into the Gulf of Mexico. This has helped make New Orleans one of the largest and busiest ports in the United States.

The Gulf of Mexico has a rich supply of fish and shellfish, including flounder, sea trout, shrimp, oysters, and crabs. Oil is another major natural resource of the Gulf. The Gulf States and Mexico pump oil from beneath the Gulf's shallow coastal waters.

Warm winds off the Gulf of Mexico sometimes bring storms with heavy rains across the eastern United States and the islands of

The Gulf of Mexico has warm waters good for fishing and for vacationers.

shrimp

the Caribbean. Very powerful storms called *hurricanes* form in the Gulf in late summer and early fall. Hurricanes may cause a great deal of damage. (*See* **hurricane.**)

The Gulf Stream, a swift current of ocean water that helps warm the climate as far away as northern Europe, is named for the Gulf of Mexico. It was once thought that the Gulf Stream began in the Gulf of Mexico. (*See* **Gulf Stream.**)

Gulf Stream

The Gulf Stream is a warm ocean current that begins in the Caribbean Sea. It flows north along the eastern coast of the United States and then across the Atlantic Ocean, toward Europe. The Gulf Stream affects the climate of western Europe, too, making winters less harsh. It also helps to create some of the world's best fishing on the Grand Banks, off the coast of Newfoundland.

Two ocean currents, called the *equatorial currents,* join to form the Gulf Stream. One current flows west across the Atlantic from southwest Africa and enters the Caribbean Sea. The other current flows west from northern Africa. Between Florida and Cuba, the two currents meet, and the Gulf Stream is born.

Near Florida, the Gulf Stream is about 80 kilometers (50 miles) wide. Besides being warmer, the waters of the Gulf Stream are bluer and saltier than the waters that surround it. If you are in a boat traveling east from Miami, you can see the water change. Then you know you are in the Gulf Stream. At this point, the Gulf Stream is flowing north toward Cape Hatteras, North Carolina, at a speed of about 5 kilometers (3 miles) per hour.

North of Cape Hatteras, the Gulf Stream becomes wider. By the time it reaches New York, the Gulf Stream is about 500 kilometers (300 miles) wide. It is also farther away from shore than it is in the south.

Flowing north toward Canada, the Gulf Stream meets a current of cold water called

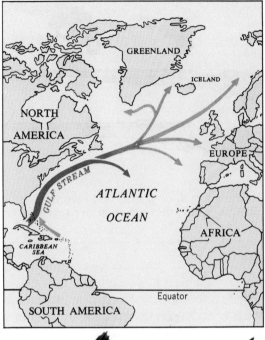

chub mackerel

The Gulf Stream carries warm waters northeast toward Europe, Iceland, and Greenland. Many fish live in its waters.

the *Labrador Current.* The two mix in the area known as the Grand Banks, south of Newfoundland. Plankton, the tiny sea creatures that fish depend on for food, thrive in this area of mixing waters. The plankton attract huge numbers of fish. This makes the Grand Banks one of the world's richest sources of fish, such as cod, haddock, herring, and mackerel.

From the Grand Banks, the Gulf Stream drifts northeast across the Atlantic. It is driven by the southwest winds that always blow in this part of the world. It moves more slowly now, at a speed of less than 8 kilometers (5 miles) per day. In midocean, it splits into several branches. One branch flows north toward Iceland. Another flows east toward Europe. A third flows south toward the Azores and the Canary Islands.

See also **ocean** and **ocean current.**

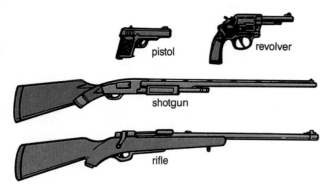

Handguns include pistols and revolvers. Shotguns and rifles are shoulder weapons.

gun

A gun is a device that propels a bullet or other object, such as a flare or dart. Most guns use a small explosion to do this. But if you have ever heard a cannon fired, the explosion may not have seemed small to you!

The first gun was invented by the Chinese over 800 years ago. It was a cannon, a gun too large to carry around. Early cannons used an explosion of gunpowder to shoot heavy balls at their targets. Today, most cannons fire shells that explode when they hit something.

The first rifle was invented in the 1400s. A *rifle* has a long tube called a *bore* through which the bullet travels. Because it is pushed by the explosion for a longer time, a bullet can go farther if it travels through a bore. Spiral grooves in the bore make the bullet spin, which makes it more likely to hit its target. Early rifles had to be reloaded every time they were fired. Most rifles today are *repeaters.* This means that they can be fired several times before they have to be reloaded.

Handguns can be held and fired with one hand. Handguns are also called *pistols.* There are two kinds of handguns—*revolvers* and *automatics.* The famed "six-shooter" of the Old West was a revolver. As each of its six bullets was fired, another one was rotated into firing position. After six shots, however, the revolver had to be reloaded. An automatic handgun, too, can be fired several

times before it has to be reloaded. Its shells are held in a *clip.* The clip automatically feeds another bullet into the gun after the previous one has been fired.

Shotguns are guns that fire many small, round pellets at the same time. These pellets are called *shot.* Shotguns are not as powerful as rifles, but they are good for hunting because the small pellets scatter. The scattered pellets may cover an area as large as 1 meter (3 feet) across.

Some guns do not use an explosion to propel their shot. *Airguns* use compressed air. Airguns are used mostly for target practice. An airgun pellet does not move as fast or travel as far as a bullet. But the pellets can be dangerous. Small game can be killed with an airgun. Children can easily be injured by airgun pellets.

All guns are dangerous. Even unloaded guns should never be pointed at a person. All small arms should be taken apart when traveling. Guns kept at home should be locked in cases.

A beginner needs training to learn to shoot a gun safely and well.

Gutenberg looks at a sheet printed in his press. The type was inked, then *pressed* down onto the paper by pulling the lever held by the young man at left.

Gutenberg, Johannes

Johannes Gutenberg was a printer who lived in Germany in the 1400s. He invented a way to make *movable type.* Movable type has a separate piece of metal for each letter.

Before Gutenberg's invention, books had to be copied page by page in handwriting. This made them so expensive that only libraries and rich people could afford them.

In Gutenberg's time, printers would cut a picture or words into a block of wood. They then rubbed ink over the block and pressed it against a sheet of paper. Many copies could be made. But to print a book meant carving many blocks.

Gutenberg made metal type for each letter. He put the letters together to make lines of words. By locking many lines together, he made up a page. After a page was printed, he could take it apart and use the type again.

Gutenberg's most famous book was a Bible, which he finished about 1456. He printed about 200 copies. More than 40 of them are still in existence.

Printers throughout Europe soon were using movable type. Movable type made books more plentiful and less expensive.

Guyana, *see* South America

gymnastics

Gymnastics are acrobatic exercises. Somersaults and cartwheels are simple gymnastics. Circus performers who twist and turn in midair are doing more difficult gymnastics. But we usually use the word *gymnastics* for the sport in which gymnasts compete. Gymnasts do a series of exercises on various pieces of special equipment. Their routines require great skill. Top gymnasts practice hundreds of hours to make their movements look graceful and easy. Yet most of the world's best gymnasts are very young—some only 12 or 13 years old.

History of Gymnastics Gymnastics is one of the oldest known sports. It is believed that Chinese soldiers did gymnastics to prepare for battle about 5,000 years ago. The Egyptians carved pictures of gymnastic exercises on the walls of their tombs about 4,000 years ago. In ancient Greece, gymnastics were an important part of a young man's training. The word *gymnastics* comes from a Greek word that means "to exercise."

Three women's events: floor exercise (left),
uneven parallel bars (above left),
and the balance beam (above). The fourth
women's event is the vault.

The modern sport of gymnastics was developed by a German teacher named Friedrich Jahn in the early 1800s. Jahn organized gymnastic clubs and competitions. The exercise equipment that gymnasts use today is modeled after equipment built by Jahn for his students. Gymnastic events were included in the Olympic Games in 1896—the year the first modern Olympics were held.

Gymnastics Today The sport of gymnastics as it is practiced today is divided into men's events and women's events. Men perform in six events—floor exercises or "tumbling," the vault, the rings, the pommel horse, the high bar, and the parallel bars.

Women compete in four events—the balance beam, the uneven parallel bars, the vault, and the floor exercises.

In the high-bar event, men swing around a horizontal bar about 108 inches (277 centimeters) above the floor. They cannot stop moving while they perform this event. Men also perform swinging movements on the parallel bars—two long wooden bars about 65 inches (165 centimeters) high and about shoulder width apart.

The ring event uses two wood rings hanging from cords attached to the gymnasium ceiling. The men perform various exercises, including handstands, while holding the rings almost perfectly still.

Two men's events: the parallel bars (left) and the rings (right). Other mens' events are floor exercise, vault, high bar, and pommel horse.

The pommel horse is actually a padded stand about 50 inches (127 centimeters) high. Two handles, called *pommels,* are in the middle of the stand. The men hold the handles to balance their weight. Then they swing their legs around the sides and top of the horse and between their hands.

In the uneven-parallel-bars event, women swing and do flips on two wooden bars—one about 90 inches (228 centimeters) high and the other 60 inches (152 centimeters) high. For the balance-beam competition, women perform movements, such as jumps and cartwheels, on a piece of wood about 144 inches (369 centimeters) long and only 4 inches (10 centimeters) wide.

In the floor exercise, a gymnast runs, somersaults, and does acrobatic leaps. The floor exercise is performed on a large mat on the gymnasium floor.

In the vault, gymnasts make acrobatic leaps over a padded stand like a pommel horse without handles. The stand is about 48 inches (123 centimeters) high.

Television coverage of the Olympic Games has made gymnastics a very popular sport. Famous Olympic gymnasts have included Olga Korbut of the Soviet Union, Nadia Comaneci of Romania, and Mary Lou Retton of the United States. Kurt Thomas and Bart Conner of the United States were both world-champion gymnasts.

67

Gypsies

The Gypsies are people who have wandered throughout the world for nearly 1,000 years. Experts think that Gypsies left northern India around the year 1000. Gypsies speak a language called Romany that is something like languages spoken today by peoples in northern India.

No one is really sure how many Gypsies there are, but there may be 3 or 4 million in all. Gypsies have been treated harshly in many countries. During World War II, about 500,000 Gypsies were killed by Nazi forces.

Many Gypsies do not stay long in one place. For this reason, they often do not vote, serve in the armed forces, or pay taxes. They have their own tight-knit communities and a rich culture. In addition to their own language, they have their own religion, traditions, and system of justice.

Gypsies are known for their exciting music and dancing. Their music may be very gay or very sad, and is usually played on violins, guitars, tambourines, and concertinas. Gypsy women often dress in bright colors and wear long, full skirts. Some are fortune-tellers. People visit them to ask what will happen in the future. Men and women alike wear a lot of gold jewelry. Many Gypsy men are skilled at working with copper, tin, and other metals.

gyroscope

A gyroscope (JYE-ro-scope) is a special instrument that spins. A toy gyroscope looks like a top in a metal frame. When the wheel in the middle is spinning, the frame will balance on a tightly stretched string or on the rim of a glass without falling off.

Gyroscopes have many important uses in transportation. They have motors that keep the center wheel spinning rapidly for long periods of time. Once the gyroscope is set to point in a particular direction, it continues pointing in that direction as long as its center is spinning.

Gyroscopes are used in the most accurate compasses on ships and planes. They continue to point north even in an airplane that is doing spins or in a ship that is tossing in a stormy sea. In fact, gyroscopes can be used to keep ships from rolling and pitching in huge ocean waves. They also help keep guns steady in warships and airplanes.

Perhaps the most interesting use of gyroscopes is in an *automatic pilot,* a device that can control a plane and keep it on course. The gyroscopes can detect any change in the plane's position. If the nose points up or down, or if the wing tilts, the gyroscopes "know." They are connected to electrical devices that move the controls to keep the plane pointed in the right direction.

A spinning gyroscope always points in the same direction. In an aircraft, a gyroscope tells a pilot when the plane is diving, climbing, or turning.

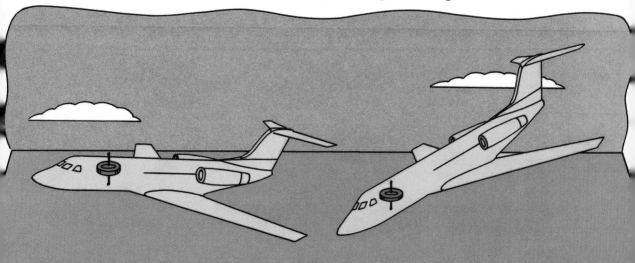

Ancient Semites and Phoenicians wrote the letter *H* like a ladder with three rungs.

The Greeks called this letter *eta* when they added it to their alphabet about 2,500 years ago.

The Romans borrowed it from the Greeks and gave it the shape and sound we know today.

hail

During some thunderstorms, you may have heard little balls of ice clattering against your window. This is hail.

Water vapor that cools high in the sky becomes tiny water drops. These tiny drops form clouds. Sometimes, instead of falling to the ground as rain, the drops are flung high into the cloud by strong winds. There, the air is cold enough to freeze the drops into ice. As the ice drops fall, they enter a warmer part of the cloud. Another layer of water forms around them. Again, strong winds fling them upward. The new water layer freezes. The ice drops grow larger.

Hail is rain that has been frozen in icy air high above the Earth (left). Below, some hailstones are as big as a baseball!

Over and over, the ice drops are swept up and fall down. When they become too heavy to be pushed up again, they fall to the ground. The largest ones do not melt on the way down. They land as hail. (*See* **thunderstorm** and **cloud**.)

Most hailstones are about the size of a pea. They usually do not do much damage. Yet, in a hailstorm with high winds, pea-size hail can flatten crops and break windows. Hailstones the size of baseballs have been found, too. Baseball-size hailstones can kill animals and people.

hair

All mammals have hair. Most mammals, such as dogs and bears, have thick coats of hair over most of their bodies. We sometimes call this their *fur*. Hair protects animals against sun, cold, and rain. A few mammals, such as whales, have almost no hair.

Like other mammals, humans have hair over their bodies. Most of it is nearly invisible. We usually think of our hair as being on top of our heads. But eyebrows and eyelashes are hair, and so is a man's beard.

Each hair grows from a group of living cells under the skin, called the hair's *root*. The root pushes the hair up through the skin. By the time the hair reaches the skin's surface, its cells have hardened and died. The part of the hair we see is called the *shaft*. Since the cells of the shaft are dead, it does not hurt to get your hair cut.

The shape of the shaft determines whether hair is straight, wavy, or curly. Straight hair

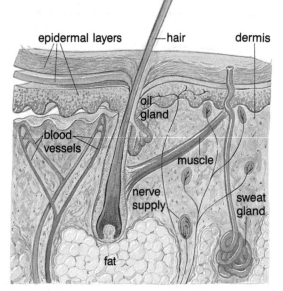

epidermal layers — hair — dermis

oil gland

blood vessels

muscle

nerve supply

sweat gland

fat

In this magnified drawing, a single hair grows out of the skin.

is round. Wavy hair is oval. Curly and frizzy hair is shaped like a flattened oval.

Human hair can grow more than a centimeter (½ inch) in a month. Hair keeps growing until it is cut or falls out. A human hair lasts about four years before it falls out. We may lose 100 hairs in a day, but new hairs take their places.

Hair that falls out is sometimes not replaced. When people lose most of the hair on their heads, we say they are *bald*.

Haiti

Capital: Port-au-Prince
Area: 10,714 square miles (27,750 square kilometers)
Population (1985): about 5,762,000
Official language: French

Haiti is a small tropical country that covers the western end of the island of Hispaniola. Haiti's neighbor, the Dominican Republic, takes up the eastern part of the island. The two countries are part of a long string of island nations called the West Indies. These islands separate the Atlantic Ocean from the Caribbean Sea. (*See* **West Indies**.)

70

Haiti is covered with mountains. In fact, its name comes from an Indian word that means "high ground." Arawak Indians were living on Hispaniola when Christopher Columbus arrived in 1492. The Spanish settlers treated the Indians harshly, and most of the Arawak died as a result. The Spanish then brought black slaves from Africa to look for gold and raise crops.

By the late 1600s, most of the Spanish had left Haiti for colonies in Mexico and South America. The French then came to Haiti and set up plantations for growing coffee and spices. The French brought more African slaves to work on the plantations. In

A busy market in Port-au-Prince, the capital of Haiti.

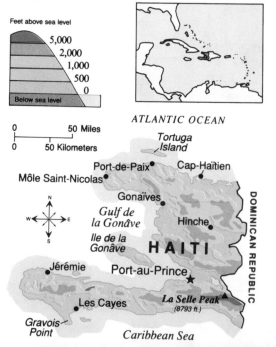

Feet above sea level

5,000
2,000
1,000
500
0
Below sea level

ATLANTIC OCEAN

0   50 Miles
0   50 Kilometers

Tortuga Island

Port-de-Paix · Cap-Haïtien

Môle Saint-Nicolas ·

Gonaïves ·

Gulf de la Gonâve

Hinche ·

Ile de la Gonâve

HAITI

Jérémie · Port-au-Prince ★

DOMINICAN REPUBLIC

Les Cayes ·

La Selle Peak (8793 ft.)

Gravois Point

Caribbean Sea

1791, Haitian slaves, led by Toussaint L'Ouverture, revolted and forced the French to leave. Haiti won complete independence from France in 1804. It was the second country in the Americas to win its freedom. The United States was the first.

Most Haitians today are descended from the African slaves brought over by the Europeans. The people live mainly along the coastal areas or in the mountain valleys. Most Haitians are poor. They live in small huts and grow their own food on small family farms. Many practice *voodoo*—a religion that combines Christian and African beliefs. Few can read or write. Educated, wealthy Haitians speak French. Most of the people, however, speak Creole, a language based on French and Spanish.

Haiti has only a few small factories. Sugarcane and coffee are grown on large plantations and sold to other countries. A few people work in hotels in Haiti's capital and largest city, Port-au-Prince.

Haiti is a republic, with a constitution and a legislature. But since becoming independent, Haiti has been ruled mostly by leaders more interested in power than in helping the people. As a result, Haiti is one of the poorest countries in the Americas. Life is so hard that many Haitians have left to live in the United States and other countries.

Halloween

Halloween is a holiday celebrated on the night of October 31—All Hallows' Eve. The day that follows, November 1, is All Hallows' Day, a Christian festival honoring all saints.

The rituals of Halloween began with the Celts 2,000 years ago, in what are now Great Britain, Ireland, and France. The Celts' New Year fell on November 1. On the evening before, the Celts honored the god of death. They believed that the souls of the dead were allowed to visit their earthly homes for that one evening. Later, in Europe during Medieval times, people believed that witches flew on that night. We still tell stories about

A girl dresses in a costume for Halloween. Pumpkin faces are part of the holiday fun.

ghosts and witches and pretend that goblins play Halloween pranks.

As part of their new-year celebration, the Celts built bonfires and dressed in animal costumes. They told fortunes about the coming year. Today, in the United States, people put lighted candles inside carved pumpkins called jack-o'-lanterns. People dress in costumes. They go to parties, tell fortunes, and bob for apples. Some children go out trick-or-treating from door to door. Sometimes they play tricks, if they do not get treats.

See also **Celts.**

Hamilton, Alexander

Alexander Hamilton was a political leader who greatly influenced the United States during its early years. Hamilton attended the Constitutional Convention in 1787. Afterward, he worked to get the Constitution approved by the states.

Hamilton was born in the British West Indies in 1755. At age 11, he went to work for a trading company. His employers helped send him to college in North America. During the Revolutionary War, he left school to fight against the British. He became an assistant to General George Washington.

Hamilton believed the Constitution would strengthen the government and help the young country survive. With James Madison and John Jay, he wrote a series of newspaper articles explaining the Constitution and urging people to support it. These articles were collected in a book called *The Federalist Papers*. Later, as secretary of the Treasury under President George Washington, Hamilton persuaded the government to set up a national bank.

Hamilton died in 1804, after a pistol duel with his political enemy, Aaron Burr.

See also **Constitution of the United States.**

hamsters and gerbils

Hamsters and gerbils are small, furry animals. They are popular pets. They are clever, fun to watch, and small enough to sit in the palm of your hand. Hamsters and gerbils are also easy to care for.

Pet hamsters and gerbils live in cages. Sometimes, people let them out of the cages to pet them. It is important not to let the animals escape. They can easily get lost.

If you own a hamster or gerbil, you will need to feed it and give it fresh water once a day. Hamsters and gerbils eat nuts and seeds. They also like fruit, lettuce, and other vegetables. The cage should contain wood shavings or other material that the animals can use to make nests.

Hamsters and gerbils are rodents. Like mice and other rodents, they have large incisor teeth for gnawing. They like to gnaw on wood and other hard objects. (*See* **rodent.**)

All the pet hamsters in the world are descendants of a single family of golden hamsters that were found in Syria in 1930. Hamsters have very short tails. Inside their cheeks are large pouches. Hamsters stuff

The gerbil is a desert animal that has become a popular, easy-to-care-for pet.

food into the pouches until their cheeks puff up like balloons. The hamsters put the food in a hiding place and look for it later, when they get hungry.

Hamsters are active at night. They like to sleep during the day. They will bite if they are frightened or unhappy. Only one hamster should be kept in each cage. The cage should contain an exercise wheel. Hamsters need lots of exercise. If they cannot exercise, they will get sick.

The gerbil has a long, furry tail with a tassel at the end. It does not have cheek pouches. Gerbils are very tame and friendly. They like to be held and petted, and they like to live in groups. At least two gerbils should be kept together in a cage.

Gerbils are active at all times of the day and night. They run around and eat for a while, then sleep for a while, then are active again. Like hamsters, they need exercise. Gerbils like to dig tunnels. They also like to run in wheels. Only solid plastic wheels should be used in a gerbil cage. A gerbil might catch and hurt its tail if it runs in a wheel that has bars.

handicap

When a person is blind, or deaf, or cannot control certain muscles, or is missing an arm or a leg, we say that the person has a handicap. Some people have another kind of handicap—a *mental handicap*—that makes it hard for them to understand some kinds of information or to learn some skills.

People with handicaps often have trouble doing everyday things that others do without thinking. For example, a blind person may have trouble crossing streets. A deaf person cannot talk on the telephone. People in wheelchairs cannot climb steps. A person without an arm has trouble dressing and undressing. A person with a mental handicap may not be able to read or write.

In many times and places, handicapped people have been treated very cruelly. Today, we know that people with handicaps can lead active and exciting lives. Inventions have helped many handicapped people. Hearing aids can help a person who is nearly deaf. Artificial legs and mechanical hands can help those who have lost an arm or a leg. Wheelchairs with motors help people with crippled legs get around faster.

Most new schools, libraries, and other public buildings are built so that handicapped people can use them. There are ramps for wheelchairs. Public telephones, sinks, and drinking fountains are low enough for people in wheelchairs to reach.

Some people are trained to help handicapped people learn how to help themselves. Hospitals often have workers who teach handicapped people how to use muscles that are still strong. For example, a person whose legs are crippled may be taught exercises to strengthen muscles in the upper part of the body. Strong upper-body muscles help the person to get around more easily.

The deaf learn to speak and to understand sign language. Many television programs include sign language so the deaf can "listen." They can also get special attachments for their television sets that print out what people are saying. (*See* **sign language.**)

The blind can read by using *braille*—an alphabet of raised dots—or by listening to recorded tapes. Many blind students go to high school and college. (*See* **braille.**)

People with mental handicaps may go to special classes or to special schools. There, teachers can give them extra attention and encouragement.

Many people have not let handicaps stop them from living full lives and doing important things. Franklin Roosevelt, crippled by polio, became president of the United States.

At left, a group of deaf children talk to each other in sign language.
At right, a boy dribbles a ball from his wheelchair.

The *menorah* (candleholder) and the *dreidel* (a top) are symbols of Hanukkah.

Hanukkah

Hanukkah is a joyful Jewish festival. In English, it is called the Festival of Lights, the Festival of Dedication, or the Feast of the Maccabees. Hanukkah begins on the evening before the 25th day of the Hebrew month of Kislev—usually in December or late November. It is celebrated for eight days.

The holiday celebrates the time in 165 B.C. when Judah Maccabee and his brothers took back the Jewish Temple in Jerusalem. The Jews had been conquered three years before by the Syrians. Led by King Antiochus, the Syrians tried to make the Jews stop practicing their religion. The Syrians placed idols in the Temple and tried to force the Jews to pray to them.

After the Maccabees and their followers took the Temple back, they threw out the idols, cleaned the temple, and dedicated it again to God. They found only a small amount of oil for burning the light at the altar. But by some miracle, that small amount burned for eight days.

Jews celebrate Hanukkah by lighting the candles in a special candleholder called a *menorah.* The menorah has places for eight candles, plus an extra candle called a *shammash,* which means "servant." The shammash is used to light the other candles. On

the first night of Hanukkah, one candle is lit, on the second night, another candle is lit, and so on, until all eight candles are lit. In ancient times, people used oil lamps instead of candles.

During Hanukkah, it is a custom to give coins to children. People today often give each other presents and send cards.

Another Hanukkah custom is to eat foods cooked in oil. Some favorite Hanukkah foods are potato pancakes and doughnuts.

There is also a Hanukkah game played with a spinning top called a *dreidel.* The dreidel has four Hebrew letters, one on each side. Players compete for money or candy by following the instructions each letter stands for. The letters really stand for four Hebrew words meaning "A great miracle happened there." Some people think the miracle was that the oil lasted eight days. Others think the miracle was that a small army led by the Maccabees defeated one of the largest armies of the time. Still others think that the miracle was getting the Temple back.

harbors and ports

A harbor is a sheltered body of water that protects ships from strong wind and waves. It must be deep enough so ships will not hit bottom. It must also be wide enough for

San Francisco Bay is a good natural harbor. Ships there are safe from storms and can find good places to load and unload goods.

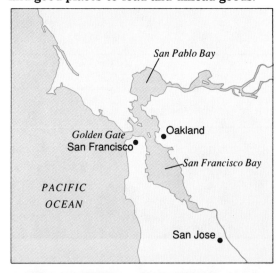

ships to sail in easily. A harbor can be natural or man-made.

A natural harbor can be in a deep bay that is part of the ocean. Ships enter a bay through a channel that connects it to the ocean. The land surrounding a bay protects it from the wind and keeps the water calm. A large bay can be lined with many docks, where hundreds of ships can park. Two well-known bays that have harbors are San Francisco Bay in California and Chesapeake Bay in Maryland.

The *mouth* of a river—where a river flows into the sea—can be a harbor. The river banks block the ocean's high waves and winds. New York City, London, New Orleans, and many other cities have important harbors because they are on large rivers.

The harbor for Los Angeles is man-made. It was made by building a 9-mile (14.5-kilometer) wall into the ocean. The wall—called a *breakwater*—blocks the large ocean waves to make waves in the harbor smaller.

A port is a place where goods and people are loaded on and off ships. A port must have docks where the ships can tie up. It must be close to roads and railroad tracks so the goods and people can reach the port. A port will have large warehouses for storing the goods. More than 3 billion tons of goods are traded through ports each year.

A port can be on a harbor, along a river, or on a lake. Several American and Canadian ports are on the Great Lakes.

Harding, Warren G., *see* presidents of the U.S.

---

hardwood tree

The two main kinds of trees are broadleaf trees and evergreen trees. Each kind of tree produces a different kind of wood. The wood of broadleaf trees has many *fibers*—long cells with thick walls. These long cells make the wood very hard, so it is called *hardwood*. You probably know of many hardwood trees—oaks, maples, walnuts, hickories, and ashes.

The wood of evergreen trees does not contain fibers. It is called *softwood*. The softwood trees you may know include pines, spruces, and cedars.

Wood from both kinds of trees is used by people. Softwood lumber is used to build the frames of houses. Softwood trees are also used to make paper and other products. Hardwood is strong and lasts a long time. It is used to make things that must hold up under a lot of wear and tear.

Hardwood floors are made from oak and maple wood. These woods lay flat and do not

A red maple (left) and an oak (right) are two trees of the hardwood family.

easily wear down when people walk on them. Good furniture is often made from oak, maple, or black walnut. These woods are sturdy and beautiful. Baseball bats, oars, and the handles of wooden tennis racquets are made from white ash. This wood can be made into long, thin objects without splitting or breaking. Hard maple can be cut and shaped into round and curved objects without splitting. This wood is used for bowling pins and croquet balls. Wooden skis are made from hickory wood. Hickory is also used for the handles of tools such as hammers and axes. Objects made from hickory can take a lot of pounding without breaking. Barrels are made from white oak because liquids do not leak through this wood.

Hardwood trees are not valued just for their wood. Many people grow hardwood trees for their beauty and for the shade they provide. Squirrels and many kinds of birds make their homes in hardwood trees.

harmony

Harmony is one of the three main parts of music. The other two are melody and rhythm. Harmony is what we hear when two or more notes are being sung or played at the same time. Nearly all music—popular music and classical music—uses harmony.

A singer can sing only one note at a time. Some instruments—such as flutes, trumpets, and clarinets—can play only one note at a time. They play in harmony only when they play with other voices or instruments.

Other instruments can play more than one note at a time. These instruments can play harmony all by themselves. Pianos and organs can play many notes together. Guitars can play many notes at almost the same instant. Violins can play two notes together. Often these instruments provide the harmony while singers or other instruments play a melody. (*See* **melody.**)

Two or more notes played together are called a *chord.* Music students learn about chords with three notes apiece. In written music, chords often look like stacks of notes, one above the other.

Many simple songs need only three chords for harmony. One of these chords is the home chord. In the key of C, the notes of this chord are C, E, and G. It is called a *1 chord* because it starts on the first note of the scale. A simple song usually ends with the 1 chord.

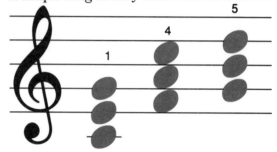

These three chords provide the harmony for many simple songs.

The other two chords are the 4 chord (F, A, and C) and the 5 chord (G, B, and D). The 5 chord is usually the next-to-last chord in a simple song. When we hear it, we want to hear the 1 chord so that the song will sound "finished."

Jazz and modern classical music use many complicated harmonies. When a chord sounds "bad" to our ears, we say it is *dissonant.* When a chord sounds good, we say it is *consonant.* In some music, dissonant chords and consonant chords come one after the other. But in some other music, most of the chords sound dissonant until we get used to them.

Harrison, Benjamin, *see* presidents of the U.S.

Harrison, William Henry, *see* presidents of the U.S.

Harvey, William

William Harvey was an English doctor who lived from 1578 to 1657. He discovered how blood moves through the body.

Other scientists of Harvey's time thought that blood was sent to the organs by the liver and the heart. They thought the organs used up the blood, and that the heart and liver always had to make a new supply. Harvey did not believe this. He discovered that the heart pumps about 19,000 liters (5,000 gallons) of blood in one day.

Harvey showed that all blood is sent out by the heart and then returns to it. Because the blood moves in a circle, the process is called *circulation.* Harvey did many experiments to prove his theory of blood circulation. By tying off blood vessels, he could observe which way blood flows through arteries and veins. In arteries, the blood collected on the side closest to the heart. In veins, blood collected on the other side. This showed that blood flows from the heart through arteries, and back to the heart through veins.

Harvey tested all of his theories by doing experiments and observing the results.

See also **blood circulation; heart;** and **experiment.**

hat

A hat is a kind of covering for the head. A true hat has a *crown* to cover the top of the head and a *brim* that circles the crown. But many head coverings without brims—such as berets, beanies, and turbans—are also called hats.

The first hats were probably worn as protection against the weather. Fur hats kept heads and ears warm. Large-brimmed hats shaded the eyes in hot, sunny climates. Many people still wear these kinds of hats for protection. People today also wear other kinds of protective hats. Hard hats protect construction workers. Helmets protect ballplayers and motorcycle riders.

We can recognize police officers, nurses, and military people by their hats. Like crowns worn by kings and queens, their hats "announce" their jobs. The saying "He wears many hats" means the person does many jobs.

Hats can protect people, show what jobs they have, or serve as decoration.

Hats are also worn for decoration. Some women's hats have colorful ribbons, veils, feathers, or artificial flowers.

Hat styles change over the years. George Washington wore a *tricorne.* Its brim came to three points. In this century, a soft felt *fedora* became popular with men. The knitted "watch cap" became a favorite with both young people and adults in the 1970s.

See also **clothing** and **fashion.**

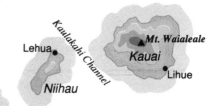

Kaulakahi Channel

Lehua•

Niihau

Kauai

▲Mt. Waialeale

Lihue

Kauai Channel

Hawaii

Capital: Honolulu
Area: 6,471 square miles (16,760 square kilometers) (47th-largest state)
Population (1980): 964,691 (1985): about 1,054,000 (39th-largest state)
Became a state: August 21, 1959 (50th state)

Hawaii is an unusual state. It is almost impossible to describe Hawaii without using the words *most* and *only.*

Land Hawaii is the only state in the United States that is not part of the North American continent. It is the southernmost and westernmost state. It is the only state completely surrounded by ocean.

Hawaii is made up of 132 islands, halfway between North America and Asia. They stretch across 1,500 miles (2,415 kilometers) of the Pacific Ocean. Almost all Hawaiians live on the eight largest islands, on the southeastern end of the chain.

Most of the Hawaiian Islands are actually the tops of underwater mountains. The mountains were active volcanoes for millions of years. Red-hot lava poured down their slopes. The lava hardened as it cooled. Rain, wind, and ocean waves gradually turned the lava rock into fertile soil.

The temperatures on the largest Hawaiian islands seldom go above 85° F (29° C) or below 60° F (16° C) near the seashore, where most of the people live. Yet there is enough snow for skiing on Mauna Kea, the state's tallest mountain.

A steady breeze usually blows from the northeast. As it crosses the ocean, it picks up moisture. When it hits the mountain slopes, the air is forced upward, where it is cooler. The cooled air cannot hold as much moisture, so the water falls as rain. More rain

falls on Mount Waialeale, on the island of Kauai, than on any other place in the world: 460 inches (1,150 centimeters) a year.

The state takes its name from its largest island, the island of Hawaii. It lies farthest to the southeast, and is known as the "Big Island." It covers 4,038 square miles (10,458 square kilometers), more than all the other Hawaiian Islands combined.

Hawaii's only active volcanoes are on the island of Hawaii. Mauna Loa is 13,680 feet (4,176 meters) high and erupts once every three or four years. Kilauea is smaller and erupts more often. In recent years, many homes have been destroyed by lava.

Sugarcane is grown on the Big Island. More orchids are grown there than anywhere else in the United States. Cattle ranching is important, too.

The island of Oahu is home to almost four-fifths of the state's population. Honolulu, the capital city, is on Oahu. Popular tourist attractions around Honolulu include Waikiki Beach, the naval station at Pearl Harbor, and Iolani Palace, the only royal palace in the United States.

History The first Hawaiians came by canoe from the Polynesian island of Tahiti, about 1,200 years ago. The first European to visit Hawaii was the British explorer Captain James Cook, in 1778. Soon, other Europeans and then Americans came. Almost three-quarters of the native Hawaiians were killed by the diseases, guns, and alcoholic drinks brought by the newcomers.

The Europeans and Americans took control of huge amounts of land. Many laborers were needed to work on their sugarcane and pineapple plantations and on their cattle and sheep ranches. Workers were brought from China, Japan, the Philippines, Portugal, and other countries.

Americans were the most powerful group by 1893. They arranged a treaty so that

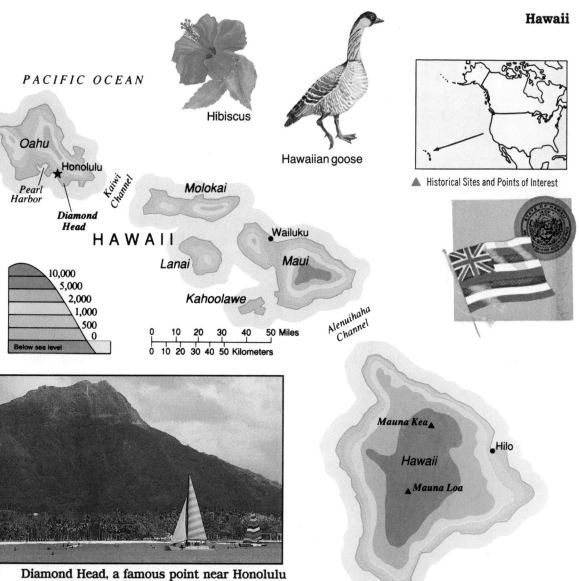

PACIFIC OCEAN

Hibiscus

Hawaiian goose

▲ Historical Sites and Points of Interest

Oahu

Honolulu ★

Pearl Harbor

Diamond Head

Kaiwi Channel

H A W A I I

Molokai

Wailuku

Lanai

Maui

Kahoolawe

Alenuihaha Channel

10,000
5,000
2,000
1,000
500
0
Below sea level

0 10 20 30 40 50 Miles
0 10 20 30 40 50 Kilometers

Mauna Kea ▲

Hilo

Hawaii

Mauna Loa ▲

Diamond Head, a famous point near Honolulu on the island of Oahu.

Hawaii could send sugar and other products to the United States without paying the usual tax. In return, Hawaii let the United States use Pearl Harbor as a naval station.

But the United States wanted political control as well as economic control. Fighting broke out, and the Hawaiian queen was forced to give up her throne. Hawaii was an independent republic for a few years, but in 1900 it became a U.S. Territory.

Japan bombed the Pearl Harbor naval base on December 7, 1941. That brought the United States into World War II. (*See* **World War II** and **Pearl Harbor.**)

After World War II, the growth of airplane travel made Hawaii easier to reach. Millions of tourists visited the beautiful islands. Thousands stayed there. Hawaii became the newest state in 1959.

People Hawaii's people are of many nationalities. About one-fourth are white, and about another one-fourth are of Japanese descent. There are many Filipinos and Chinese. About one-fifth are native Hawaiians. (*See* **Hawaiian islanders.**)

Most Hawaiians make a living by growing and processing sugarcane and pineapples, or by working on or supplying military bases. Tourism is a very important industry.

Aloha means both "welcome" and "farewell" in Hawaiian, and Hawaii is nicknamed "The Aloha State."

Queen Liliuokalani ruled Hawaii until 1893.

Hawaiian islanders

Hawaiian islanders were the first people to live in Hawaii. They came to Hawaii by canoe from Tahiti and other islands in the western Pacific Ocean that make up Polynesia.

The first Hawaiian islanders probably arrived around the year 800—about 1,200 years ago. In their canoes, they brought plant roots and seeds, dogs, pigs, and chickens. The islanders worshiped many gods. They believed the god Maui pulled Hawaii from the bottom of the sea by using a magic fishhook made from the jawbone of his grandmother.

When the first Europeans came to Hawaii in the late 1700s, there were about 225,000 Hawaiian islanders. They were ruled by many different chiefs. In 1810, a warrior named Kamehameha became Hawaii's first king. After Queen Liliuokalani lost power in 1893, Hawaii had no more kings or queens. Hawaii became a republic and was then annexed by the United States. Hawaiian islanders no longer ruled themselves.

Today, there are fewer than 10,000 pure Hawaiian islanders. Many of today's Hawaiians are descended from several peoples, including Hawaiian islanders. Hawaiian customs such as the *hula*—a dance—come from the Hawaiian islanders. The word *aloha*, which means "love" in the language of Hawaii's first people, is used in Hawaii today to mean "welcome" and "farewell."

Haydn, Franz Joseph

Franz Joseph Haydn (HIDE-n) was a great composer of music. He was born in Austria in 1732 and began composing in the 1750s. He wrote and played music for more than 50 years.

Haydn worked for a noble Austrian family who had several palaces. They paid a group of about 25 musicians to play for them year-round. Haydn was the musicians' director. He wrote a lot of the music they played.

Haydn wrote much of his music for orchestra. The orchestra in Haydn's time had most of the same instruments as today's orchestra—violins and violas, cellos and string basses, oboes and flutes, and sometimes trumpets and drums. Haydn wrote more than 100 symphonies for orchestra. His symphonies each have three or four parts, called *movements*. The first and last movements are usually fast. The second movement is slow. The third is a dance called a *minuet*.

One of Haydn's most famous symphonies is called the "Surprise." After a quiet, slow part, the whole orchestra suddenly hits a very loud note. Some people think Haydn was trying to wake up people who were falling asleep in the audience!

See also **orchestra** and **symphony**.

Haydn lived for 77 years and wrote thousands of pieces of music.

Hayes, Rutherford B., *see* presidents of the U.S.

hay fever, *see* allergy

health

Health is a state of complete physical, mental, and social well-being. When you are totally healthy, you are fit and well nourished. You feel good!

Good food, exercise, rest, and cleanliness can help boys and girls stay in good health. Friendships, work, and relaxation are also important.

Your *life-style*—the way you live—is one of the keys to good health. By following good health habits, you will be at your best. You will also decrease the risk of getting sick. Good health habits include proper nutrition, exercise, rest, cleanliness, and medical and dental care. Healthy people also know how to handle stress.

WELL-BALANCED DIET

breakfast

lunch

snack

dinner

Good meals and a healthy snack make up good nutrition.

Eating for Health A well-balanced diet provides the energy you need for all your activities. It also supplies the nutrients your body needs to grow and repair itself. A healthful diet includes a wide variety of foods. Fruits and vegetables provide important vitamins and minerals. They also help keep the digestive system healthy. Meat, eggs, fish, beans, and nuts are good sources of protein. Dairy foods, such as milk, cheese, and yogurt, are the best source of calcium. Breads and cereals provide carbohydrates.

A healthful diet includes only small amounts of fat, sugar, and salt. Eating too much salt and too many fatty foods can lead to health problems such as heart disease. Eating too much sugar can cause weight gain and tooth decay. (*See* **nutrition.**)

Exercising for Health Exercise improves physical fitness. It is also a good way to reduce stress. Most people feel a sense of well-being after a good workout. Regular exercise makes muscles, bones, and joints stronger and more flexible. But the most important benefit of exercise is its effect on the heart and lungs. With regular exercise, the heart gets stronger. It can pump more blood with each beat. The lungs supply more oxygen to the blood with each breath. All of the cells in the body benefit from a constant supply of fresh food and oxygen.

Aerobic exercises make your heart beat quickly over a long period of time. They are the most helpful exercises. Jogging, swimming, bicycling, walking, and dancing are good exercises to strengthen the heart. (*See* **aerobic exercise.**)

Exercises that build muscle strength are helpful, too. It is important to begin and end every exercise program with stretching exercises. This helps to prevent injuries and muscle soreness.

Physical fitness does not come without effort. Start an exercise program slowly. Little by little, do more and harder exercises as the body becomes more fit. What is most important is to exercise on a regular basis.

Hiking and other outdoor exercise are important to good health.

FEELINGS AND HEALTH

When people are  or *DEPRESSED*, or *AFRAID*...

they have a hard time paying attention to work or play,
they get into arguments with family and friends, and
they may get headaches, stomachaches, or other health problems.

SOME ANSWERS

1. **Knowing how we feel.**
   Sometimes we can be very angry or depressed or afraid without knowing it.

2. **Understanding how we feel.**
   We need to find out what or whom we are angry at, depressed about, or afraid of.

3. **Talking about how we feel.**
   Sometimes just talking about painful feelings with a friend or an adult makes us feel better.

4. **Dealing with our painful feelings.**
   For example, an angry person may feel less angry after kicking a football or punching a punching bag. A depressed person may feel more cheerful when playing music or doing some other favorite activity.

Rest and Health Getting the proper amount of rest and sleep is as important as getting enough exercise. Sleep is needed to restore energy to the body. During sleep, growth hormones are released into the blood. These hormones are needed for the growth and repair of body tissues. After a good night's sleep, your muscles feel relaxed and your mind is alert. (*See* **sleep.**)

Cleanliness and Health Keeping your body clean is also important for good health. Bathing keeps the body free from dirt and odor. Cleanliness prevents harmful germs from growing on the body. The hair should also be washed regularly to remove oil and dirt. The fingernails and toenails should be kept clean and well trimmed.

Are soft drinks, candy, and other sweets a regular part of your diet? If so, you are helping to cause cavities and gum diseases. Tooth decay is a common disease. Proper care of the teeth and gums can help prevent tooth decay. You should try to avoid sugary foods, especially between meals. The teeth should be brushed and flossed each day. This helps remove food particles and plaque. Good dental care also includes going to the dentist at least twice a year. (*See* **dentistry** and **teeth.**)

Other Good Health Habits To stay healthy, a person should go to a doctor for regular checkups. Your doctor will make sure you are vaccinated against diseases such as measles, mumps, polio, and tetanus. You should also get medical care if you feel really sick or have a serious accident. Early care can result in a quicker cure.

Stress can cause both mental and physical illness. It is a normal part of life. Many events can cause stress. The death of a loved one, a new baby in the family, moving, marriage, or changing schools are some events that can cause stress. People under a lot of stress feel very tense. They may have trouble falling asleep. They may have stomachaches or headaches, and allergies may become worse.

It is important to learn how to cope with stress. Some people rely on drugs, tobacco, or alcohol to relieve stress. Those people soon have even more problems to solve. The best way to handle stress is to learn positive ways to cope with it. Plan time to relax each day. Eat well and exercise regularly.

hearing

Hearing is one of our most important senses. Hearing makes it possible for us to talk and to listen to others. Hearing music gives us pleasure. Hearing lets us know what is happening around us. Close your eyes for one minute. How many different sounds can you hear? Can you tell what made these sounds? As you can see, much of our information about the outside world comes to us through our sense of hearing.

Sound and Hearing What exactly are sounds and how can we hear them? Sounds are made by anything that *vibrates*—moves back and forth very quickly. The human voice is produced when the vocal cords vibrate. Place your hand on the front of your neck. When you talk, you can feel your vocal cords vibrate. If you pluck a stretched rubber band, it begins to vibrate and makes a sound. Stringed instruments, too, produce sound in this way.

Any vibrating object causes the air around it to move. The vibrating object pushes air molecules together and then spreads them apart in a wave pattern. In other words, the

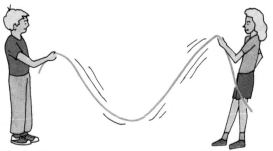

Sound travels in waves that have the same shape as a jump rope being twirled.

air molecules around the object begin to vibrate as well.

The vibrating air molecules reach your ears. Inside each ear is a *membrane*—a thin covering—called the *eardrum*. When the vibrating air molecules reach the eardrum, it begins to vibrate, too. It pushes against three tiny bones. The bones in turn push against a membrane that runs down the center of a coiled tube. The membrane is covered with tiny hairs. The hairs are connected to nerves. When the membrane is pushed, the hairs bend and the nerves "fire," sending messages to the brain. When these nerve impulses reach the brain, you hear sound.

Pitch and Amplitude Humans can hear a wide range of sounds. *Pitch* refers to the highness or lowness of a sound. Pitch is measured in *hertz*. A hertz is one single

Humans can hear sounds made by pianos, humans, dogs, cats, and birds. Humans can measure very high sounds made by bats and locusts (far right) but cannot hear them.

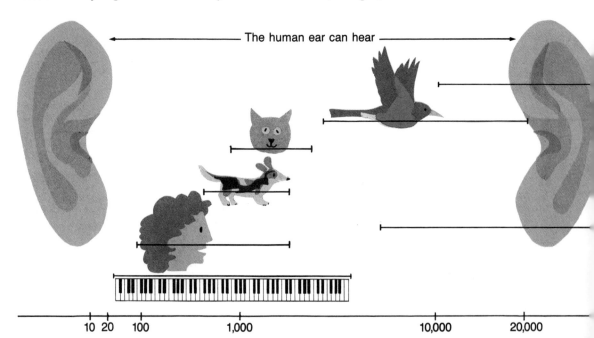

The human ear can hear

10 20   100   1,000   10,000   20,000

vibration—one back-and-forth movement —per second. The faster an object vibrates, the higher the pitch of the sound it produces. Humans can hear pitches from 20 to 20,000 hertz. This is equal to about ten octaves on a musical scale. Some animals, such as dogs, can hear pitches above the range of human hearing. This is why dogs can hear dog whistles that we call "silent."

Amplitude refers to the loudness of a sound. Amplitude is measured in *decibels*. The faintest sound the human ear can hear is 0 decibels. Talking in an ordinary tone of voice takes place at 65 decibels. Sounds begin to hurt the ears at about 100 decibels. Sounds above 120 decibels cause a pricking feeling in the ears. A jet plane taking off can produce this loud a sound. Sounds that are even louder can cause pain and loss of hearing for a short while.

How the Ear Works The human ear can detect differences in the loudness of sounds. The louder the sound, the farther in and out the eardrum vibrates. The more strongly the eardrum vibrates, the harder it pushes on the three tiny bones of the middle ear. These bones push on the membrane inside the coiled tube. The harder the middle ear bones push on this membrane, the farther back

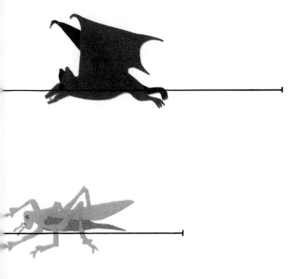

PROTECT YOUR EARS

Never put anything into your ears.
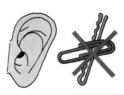

When you have a cold, do not blow your nose too hard. (It can drive an infection into your ears.)

Do not listen to loud music.
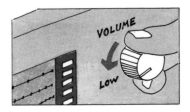

See a doctor at once if you have an ear infection.

and forth it vibrates. The farther back and forth this membrane moves, the greater the number of nerve fibers that fire, and the louder the sound that is heard.

The human ear can also detect differences in pitch. A low pitch causes the membrane inside the coiled tube to vibrate near the tip of the tube. A high pitch causes it to vibrate near the base of the coiled tube. Where the membrane vibrates, nerve cells are fired. The brain hears different pitches, depending on which nerve cells are fired.

Protecting Your Hearing Many people have some hearing loss. One cause of hearing loss is middle-ear infections. Middle-ear infections can damage the eardrum and also cause the three middle ear bones to bind together. Loud sounds can cause hearing loss, too. People who must work around loud noises should wear earmuffs. Even listening to loud music can be harmful to the ears.

Many of the people who have hearing loss can be helped. There are different kinds of hearing aids that can be used to magnify sounds. Those who are severely deaf can learn sign language and lipreading. (*See* **sign language.**)

See also **ear** and **sound.**

100,000 hertz

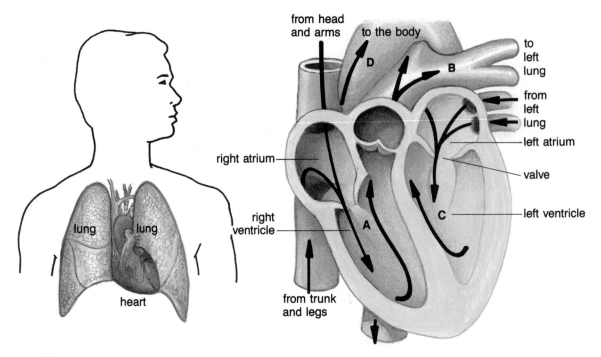

from head and arms

to the body

to left lung

from left lung

D

B

left atrium

valve

right atrium

left ventricle

right ventricle

A

C

from trunk and legs

lung

lung

heart

The heart is an amazing pump in the chest that sends blood out to the body and to the lungs. If the heart stops beating, a person can live only about ten minutes.

heart

Your heart is always beating, even when you are asleep. As long as your heart keeps beating, blood is being carried to your brain and other parts of your body. Your heart keeps you alive.

The heart is a hollow muscular organ near the center of the chest. An adult's heart is about the size of your fist and weighs about 280 grams (10 ounces).

The heart is made of thick, strong muscles. These muscles are different from the other muscles in your body. They keep working all your life without ever resting. The heart is inside a thin sac made of tough tissue. This sac protects the heart and keeps it from rubbing against the lungs.

Early scientists were not sure what the different parts of the body did. Some believed that the heart was the source of emotions, such as love, hate, fear, and jealousy. We still connect the heart with love and with bravery. But the heart really has nothing to do with emotions. It is a pump that supplies all the parts of your body with blood. The blood carries oxygen and food needed to make the body work.

The heart is actually a double pump. A wall divides it into a left half and a right half. Each half has a muscular lower room, called the *ventricle,* and a thin-walled upper room, called the *atrium.* The right atrium collects blood flowing into the heart. From here, the blood flows through a one-way valve into the right ventricle. The valve prevents the blood from flowing backward.

The right ventricle pumps the blood through a blood vessel to the lungs. There, the blood releases carbon dioxide and picks up oxygen. Then the blood flows back to the heart.

The blood enters the heart through the left atrium. From here, it flows into the left ventricle, which pumps it out to the body.

The beating of the heart responds to the needs of the body. A child's heart usually beats between 80 and 100 times a minute. When you run or swim, your heart beats faster to supply your muscles with more oxygen. When you sit quietly, your muscles need less oxygen, so your heart beats more slowly. Altogether, the average person's heart will beat about 2½ billion times during the total life span.

See also **blood circulation.**

heart disease

Heart disease is the cause of more than half of all deaths in the United States. Heart disease develops when the normal flow of blood is stopped in some way. Blood pumped from the heart carries oxygen and food to the cells. If this blood fails to reach the cells, they begin to die. Not all diseases that are called *heart disease* actually affect the heart. Diseases in other parts of the body that affect blood circulation are considered heart disease as well.

Heart attacks and *strokes* are two results of heart disease. If an artery to the heart is blocked, a heart attack may occur. The heart muscle begins to die and may no longer be able to pump blood. If an artery to the brain is blocked, a stroke may occur. Part of the brain will stop working. A stroke may also occur if a blood vessel in the brain breaks open.

The main causes of heart disease are diseased arteries and high blood pressure. Sometimes, a person is born with a heart that is not perfectly formed. Also, some diseases attack the heart and destroy heart muscle.

Blood pressure is the force with which blood pushes against blood-vessel walls as the heart pumps. High blood pressure simply means that the force is stronger than normal. There are many drugs that can lower blood pressure. Losing weight, cutting down on salt, and stopping smoking can also lower blood pressure. High blood pressure can produce strokes by causing weak spots in arteries to break open. It can also contribute to other forms of heart disease.

The arteries become diseased when fatty materials are deposited on their inside walls. These deposits narrow the arteries, so blood cannot move through them easily. A blood *clot*—a blob of thickened blood—can get caught in a narrow artery and block it off. Then the body tissue that the artery supplies cannot get enough oxygen or nutrients. When that happens, the tissue begins to die.

The arteries of the heart are especially likely to become clogged. This clogging causes the most common kind of heart attack. Most heart attacks happen to older people. Signs of a heart attack include pressure or pain in the center of the chest. Pain is often felt in the arms and shoulders, too.

Some people inherit a greater chance of developing heart disease. But some of the things that contribute to heart disease can be avoided. Smoking, eating too much (especially animal fats), lack of exercise, and worrying too much can all increase your risks of heart disease.

Today, surgeons can perform amazing kinds of heart surgery to help people survive serious heart disease. By-pass operations replace clogged or damaged arteries. A healthy human heart can be *transplanted* into a patient when the patient's own heart cannot be healed. Surgeons are also experimenting with using artificial hearts to help save the lives of patients who would die unless they received a heart transplant. (*See* **transplant.**)

To stay healthy, the heart needs exercise. Bicycling, jogging, and walking are three good kinds of activity.

heat

Everyone knows something about heat. On a hot day, people complain about too much heat. They stay indoors to keep cool. When we turn on a furnace, we sometimes say we are "turning on the heat." The heat from a stove burner will warm water in a kettle. The heat in an oven will bake a cake.

We know that adding heat to some things can make them change. If you put liquid cake batter into the heated oven, it turns into a solid. But if you put solid ice into a pan and heat it, the ice turns to water. If you keep heating the water, it will boil and seem to disappear. The heat has turned the water into an invisible gas called steam. When some other things are heated, they catch fire and burn. (*See* **fire.**)

Heat is important to humans and many other living things. Our bodies are always making heat. Our bodies use the food we eat as fuel. They "burn" it to keep our body temperature at about 37° C (98.6° F) most of the time. Sometimes, when you have an infection, your body increases your temperature. Then you have a fever.

What Is Heat? We see what heat does around us every day. But what exactly is heat?

All materials—even air and other gases—are made of tiny particles called *molecules.* These tiny particles are always moving. If a thing is very cold, the molecules in it are moving slowly. If it is very hot, the molecules are moving very quickly. Heat is the energy that make the molecules move.

Heat can travel from one material to another. For example, when you hold a mug of hot chocolate, your hands get heat from the mug and become warmer. Moving molecules in the warm mug bump into the molecules in your hand and make them move faster. The faster the molecules move, the more heat your hand has.

The heat in the warm mug moves to your hand by *conduction.* Some materials *conduct*—carry—heat well. Metals are good heat

Heat may travel through the air by radiation, through a pan by conduction, and through the water by convection.

conductors. Pans are made of metal so that food in them will get heated quickly. Other materials, such as wood, conduct heat poorly. We use wooden spoons for stirring hot food because they do not conduct heat, and so will not burn our hands.

Heat moves in a gas or a liquid by *convection.* A warm stove warms the air near the stove. As it gets warm, this air *expands*—the molecules spread out. This makes the warm air lighter, and it starts to rise toward the top of the room. As the rising air moves away from the stove, it cools and gets heavier. Then it drifts down toward the stove to be heated again. The air in the room is soon moving in a big circle called a *convection current.*

Heat also travels by *radiation.* Heat from the sun warms land, water, and air by radiation. If you sit quietly in the sun, you can feel

In solar panels (below), sunlight heats a liquid. The heated liquid is sent through pipes (right) to an energy plant.

the warmth of the sunlight where it strikes your skin. Some of the energy in sunlight changes to heat, making the molecules in your skin move faster. Radiant heat from the sun keeps the earth warm enough for most living things to stay alive.

Changing Heat Heat can be changed to other forms of energy for moving or lifting things, or doing other work. In a steam engine, we heat water. When it turns to steam, it expands, pushing hard against the boiler walls. We can use the expanding steam to make a locomotive go, or to turn huge generators that make electrical power.

Heat and Temperature Scientists often think of heat as the total amount of heat energy something has. How much heat energy it has depends on its temperature and on its size. Which has more heat energy, a cup of boiling water (100° C) or a bathtub full of

warm water (38° C)? One way to find out would be to measure how many ice cubes the two bodies of water can melt.

Even without trying the experiment, you can guess that the bathtub full of water will melt much more ice. The temperature of the boiling water is higher, but there is more heat energy in the water in the bathtub.

Scientists measure heat energy in *calories.* A calorie is the amount of energy it takes to raise the temperature of 1 cubic centimeter—*cc*—of water 1° C. People who are on diets count the heat energy in foods in calories. One food calorie is equal to 1,000 scientific calories. A food calorie is enough heat energy to raise the temperature of a liter of water (about a quart) 1° C.

HOW HOT IS HOT?

Fahrenheit   Celsius

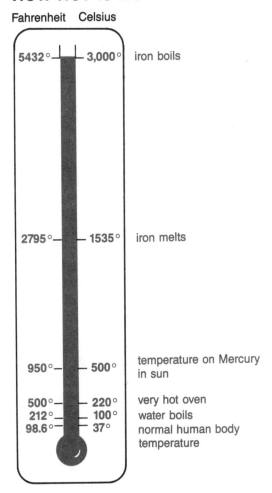

Fahrenheit	Celsius	
5432°	3,000°	iron boils
2795°	1535°	iron melts
950°	500°	temperature on Mercury in sun
500°	220°	very hot oven
212°	100°	water boils
98.6°	37°	normal human body temperature

heating and ventilation

People have heated their homes with fire for many thousands of years. Cave dwellers built large fires in the center of stone or dirt floors. People gathered around fires for warmth, but they got plenty of smoke, too. Their caves had practically no ventilation—ways for smoke to leave the caves.

When people began building simple houses, they still kept fires burning in the center of the dirt floors. But they made small openings above the fire. Some of the smoke could escape, though most of the warmth stayed in. This was the first kind of ventilated central heating system. A central heating system is one that has a single source of heat for an entire building.

The Romans improved on central heating. They built their houses with a special room, called the *atrium,* in the center. The atrium was built of stone and brick to contain a large fire. Smoke escaped from a ventilation hole, but hot air was carried to the other rooms of the house by pipes.

Fireplaces and Stoves During the Middle Ages (around A.D. 500 to 1500), homes and castles were heated by fireplaces. The first fireplaces were not like those we see today. They were built against walls, not into walls, and still used a hole in the roof for ventilation. Several centuries passed before chimneys and flues took the place of those simple holes.

By the end of the 1500s, metal stoves were being used for cooking and heating. Later, Benjamin Franklin invented the "Franklin Stove," an iron stove that could burn wood or coal. The Franklin Stove was very popular during colonial days, and stoves like it are still being made.

Metal heating stoves contain fire. They have metal doors that can be shut so less air is let in. This keeps fuel from burning too quickly. Metal is a better heat conductor than brick or stone. The walls of a metal stove *conduct*—carry—the heat of the fire into the air. A metal stove in the center of a room also *radiates* heat—sends heat out in all directions. (*See* **heat.**)

A stovepipe carries smoke from the stove to the outdoors through a hole in the roof or wall. A long stovepipe also gets hot enough to help heat the room.

Modern Central Heating Since the 1900s, most buildings have used some form of central heating system: steam, hot water, or hot air.

Steam heat begins with a *furnace*—a large metal stove. The furnace heats water in a

INDOOR HEATING

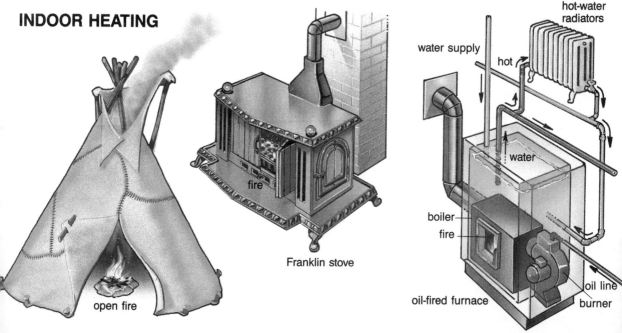

open fire

Franklin stove

fire

water supply

hot

hot-water radiators

water

boiler
fire

oil-fired furnace

oil line
burner

boiler. Pipes carry the hot steam from the boiling water to containers called *radiators* that are put in each room of the house. The radiators heat the air in the rooms by conducting and radiating.

A hot-water heating system is much like a steam system except that the water is not heated to boiling. The hot water expands—although not as much as steam—and forces its way through pipes and radiators. Most modern steam and hot-water systems use pumps to help push along the steam or hot water.

Hot-air systems also use furnaces. But instead of heating water, they heat air in a chamber. Fans, rather than pumps, force the hot air through large pipes called *ducts*. The hot air enters each room through *vents*—openings at the ends of the ducts.

Other Heating Systems Electric heating can use plug-in heaters or electrical panels built into the baseboards around the walls of rooms. Electric heaters change electrical energy into heat energy, the way a toaster does. Electric heat is not centralized. Each room has its own source of heat.

Solar heating uses energy from the sun. Some solar heating systems use special panels to absorb heat energy from the sun. This energy is used to produce hot water, steam, or hot air to warm buildings or homes. Sometimes, the building itself is designed to trap the sun's heat. Modern solar heating systems can store enough heat to last for several cloudy days. Most have backup systems of a different kind in case there are longer periods without sun.

Ventilation Systems Heating rooms or buildings is very important, but ventilation is just as important. Ventilation does more than let smoke out of a building. It keeps air circulating. A room with no ventilation becomes filled with "stale" air. Stale air is air that has had much of its oxygen used up. It is also full of dust, germs, and even water vapor from people breathing and perspiring. Poisonous chemicals in building materials can build up in unventilated air.

Ventilation is circulating air through a room or building.

The simplest way to ventilate is to open windows and use fans to pull in fresh air and push out stale air. Some ventilation systems circulate air through filters that remove dust and other particles. Some systems even wash the air. (*See* **air conditioning**.)

No matter where people live in the future—underground, under the sea, in space stations, or on other planets—they will continue to need heating and ventilation in their shelters.

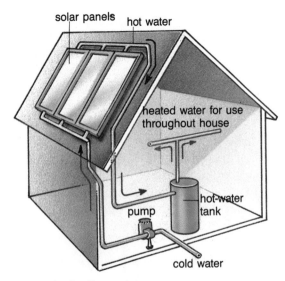

solar panels   hot water
heated water for use throughout house
pump   hot-water tank
cold water
solar heating system

Hebrews, *see* **Israelites; Judaism**

Heidi

Heidi is a children's book that first appeared in 1881. It tells the story of a girl growing up in the Alps of Switzerland. The book was written by Johanna Spyri, a Swiss author who lived from 1827 to 1901.

Heidi is five years old when her parents die. She is brought to her grandfather, who lives alone on a mountain. Heidi's grandfather is an unfriendly man who is not well liked by the townspeople. He is good to Heidi in his own gruff way, and eventually grows to love her. Her kindness changes him.

Heidi makes friends with Peter, a boy who herds goats. She visits Peter's blind grandmother every afternoon and asks her grandfather to help the old woman.

When Heidi is eight, she is taken by her cousin to live with a rich, crippled girl named Clara. During her time with Clara, Heidi learns to read. But she misses her grandfather and the mountains, and is finally allowed to return. Clara visits Heidi, and the mountain air makes her strong. Soon, she is able to walk again.

Heidi has been popular with young readers ever since it first appeared. For this reason, it is called a *classic*.

See also **children's books.**

Heidi loved life in the mountains.

A small passenger helicoper (top) is used by radio stations to report on traffic conditions. Rescue helicopters (bottom) are used as flying ambulances. The largest helicopters can carry heavy cargo (right).

helicopter

A helicopter is a special kind of aircraft. Unlike ordinary aircraft, a helicopter can move straight up and down, backwards, and to either side. It can also *hover*—stay in one spot in the air. Ordinary aircraft need a long runway to land on. But helicopters can land on small spaces—streets and lawns, tops of buildings and small fields. So they can be used to do many jobs that ordinary aircraft can't do.

Propellers on the front of an airplane pull air over the wings to keep the plane flying. Helicopters have no wings. They have only propellers called *rotors*. The main rotor lies flat on top of the helicopter. This rotor has three or four blades that act as "wings." When the helicopter's engines turn the rotor, the blades push air downward. This lifts the helicopter straight off the ground. Some helicopters have two of these rotors spinning in opposite directions.

The pilot can control the *pitch*—angle—of the rotor blades. Different pitches will cause the helicopter to rise, descend, hover, or even to turn.

Helicopters also have at least one tail rotor. It is used to help steer, much like the rudder of a boat or airplane. The tail rotor is smaller

than the main rotor. It is mounted at the rear, sideways, so that it pushes air to the right or left, rather than up or down. If the helicopter has only one main rotor, the tail rotor has another purpose as well. It keeps the cabin of the helicopter from spinning around when the main rotor turns.

Leonardo da Vinci, an Italian artist and inventor, sketched helicopter designs in the 1500s. But a really practical helicopter was not built until 400 years later. It was developed in 1939 by Igor Sikorsky, a Russian who had become a U.S. citizen.

Helicopters were used for special jobs by both sides in World War II and in the Korean War. By the 1960s, helicopters were as important to the armed forces as airplanes. Large helicopters could even carry tanks. Others were designed to rescue injured soldiers or strike enemy targets.

Helicopters have many other uses besides military ones. They are used to fight fires and to broadcast radio reports on traffic conditions. Hospitals use them to transport accident victims to places where they can get special treatment. People take passenger helicopters to work, or to get to airports quickly. Helicopters are also used to pick up astronauts when spaceships land in the ocean.

See also **aircraft** and **Leonardo da Vinci.**

helium

Helium is the second-most-common element in the universe. Yet it makes up only a small amount of the matter on Earth. Helium exists in all galaxies and stars. On Earth, it is found in the air and in places where there is natural gas. Helium is so light that it escapes from Earth's gravity into space.

Helium was discovered by a scientist as he was looking at sunlight. When light is separated into a *spectrum*—a rainbow—bright and dark lines can be seen, as well as stripes of colors. The light from each of the elements produces a different pattern of lines. In 1868, Pierre Janssen saw a new line pattern in sunlight.

Scientists thought this meant the presence of an unknown element. They named the new element *helium,* from the Greek word *helios,* which means "sun." Almost 30 years later, a scientist named William Ramsay saw the same lines in the spectrum produced by an unknown gas found in a mine. That gas, too, was helium.

Helium does not burn or combine easily with other elements. It is used in place of an air layer to prevent dangerous chemicals from catching fire or exploding. Large balloons are filled with helium instead of hydrogen, which is lighter but can burn.

See also **element; gas;** and **balloon.**

This blimp is lighter than air because it is filled with helium.

Henry, John

John Henry is a legendary figure in America, a black worker who figures in ballads, folk stories, and work songs. He is the famous "steel-driving man" who competed with a machine and won—for a little while.

A *steel-driving man* was someone who pounded a steel drill into rock with a long-handled hammer, making deep holes. Then explosives were dropped into the holes and set off. In this way, tunnels needed for the railroads were blown out of the hard rock of mountains.

John Henry's contest was said to have taken place in West Virginia. Steel drivers were working there on the Big Bend Tunnel for the Chesapeake and Ohio Railroad. Everyone knew John Henry was as strong as 20 men. So when a city slicker claimed that his steam steel-driving machine could beat any human being, John Henry's boss said, "Want to bet?"

John Henry and the machine worked all day, drilling harder than either were used to. At the end of many hours, the machine

John Henry was a legendary hero who won a contest against a steam-driven machine.

broke down. John Henry smiled. He looked around, then gave one last pound with his great hammer. The crowd cheered. John Henry beat the machine fair and square.

The boss was collecting his bet from the steam drill owner when someone noticed that John Henry didn't look good. Sure enough, poor John Henry had broken down, too. He was so worn out from his effort to beat the machine that he died then and there, with the hammer in his hand.

It is possible that a real John Henry was alive around 1870, when the Big Bend Tunnel was being built. The steam steel-driving engine had just been invented. Many old-timers claimed that there was indeed a race between a powerful, hard worker like John Henry and such a machine.

John Henry is an important figure in American folk stories because he is a symbol of man in competition with the machine. John Henry stands for the dignity of a human being working by his own strength, and doing his best. The machine stands for the way the world has become—everything run by pushing buttons.

John Henry also represents the black man in America. Without the help of men like John Henry, the railroads could not have been built. But the hard work of such men was rarely appreciated.

Henry, Patrick

Patrick Henry was a famous American patriot. He was governor of Virginia during the Revolutionary War. He was a powerful speaker. His fiery words "Give me liberty or give me death" urged Virginians to fight against British rule.

Henry was born in Virginia in 1736. His talent for public speaking made him a successful lawyer. Henry was elected to Virginia's House of Burgesses in 1765. That year, the British government passed the Stamp Act, which placed a tax on all colonial newspapers, calendars, pamphlets, and legal papers. Henry spoke in the House against the

Patrick Henry gives his famous speech to the Virginia House of Burgesses.

Stamp Act and against the British king, George III. Some called his words treason against Britain. "If this be treason, make the most of it," was Henry's reply.

Henry opposed the Constitution when it was first drawn up. He thought a strong central government might not do enough to protect the rights of individuals. Partly due to his efforts, the Bill of Rights was added to the Constitution in 1791.

Henry served five terms as Virginia's governor. He later won a seat in the Virginia state legislature, but died right after the election, in 1799.

See also **Revolutionary War; Constitution of the United States;** and **Bill of Rights.**

herb

Scientists call plants without woody stems herbs. But to most people, herbs are plants with seeds, leaves, roots, or flowers that are used as medicines, flavors, or scents.

Early people believed that herbs had magical powers. Wood betony could protect you from witchcraft and nightmares. A drink made from borage flowers would give you courage. Periwinkle could make you fall in love.

As medicines, herbs are made into tea or mixed with ointment. They may also be made into *poultices*—mashed leaves or roots applied to a diseased or injured part of the body. The ancient Greeks and Romans ate licorice as a remedy for colds and coughs. The Cherokee Indians drank bitter-tasting goldenseal to relieve stomach trouble. The leaves and roots of comfrey have long been used in poultices to help heal wounds. Today, scientists still study herbs to see how they can be used as medicine.

Herbs give the cooking of each country its characteristic flavor. Aniseeds flavor many Italian pastries. French cooks use tarragon, sorrel, basil, and thyme. Turmeric and saffron give Indian food a special flavor and yellow color.

Fragrant herbs—such as lavender, lemon verbena, and bergamot—are added to soap and perfume. People place sachets of scented herbs among their clothing. Lavender, tansy, and wormwood are also used in closets to keep away moths.

Some herbs are made into tea, or give flavor to foods. Lavender can give a nice smell to a drawer or closet.

chamomile

parsley

dill

lavender

garlic

herbivore, *see* **animal**

This child inherits many qualities from her mother and grandmother (left). Some qualities do *not* depend on heredity. For example, the big goldfish (right) is larger because it lives in a larger pond and gets more to eat.

heredity

Certain characteristics seem to run in families. In some families, almost everyone has red hair. In others, everyone has brown eyes. Family members may all have dimples or button noses. We look something like our parents because of heredity.

How living things look is controlled by a chemical in their cells called DNA. When living things reproduce, an egg and a sperm join. Both pass along part of their DNA. Each egg has DNA from the mother. Each sperm has DNA from the father. This DNA contains instructions for the *traits*—qualities—of the offspring. In humans and other animals, these traits include hair color, eye color, skin color, height, and body shape. In plants, traits controlled by DNA include flower color and seed shape. Traits that pass from parents to offspring through DNA are said to be *inherited*. Inherited traits make up a living thing's heredity.

Offspring may look a lot like their parents, but they don't look exactly like either parent. They get only half of their DNA from each parent.

Some traits in the heredity of a living thing are set. For example, the number of legs and the number of wings an insect has is controlled by DNA. So is the arrangement of a cat or dog's teeth. These are traits that cannot be changed by the living thing's *environment*—surroundings.

Other inherited traits are affected by the environment. Living things inherit DNA instructions that partly control body size. But diet also plays a role. A fish that eats a lot will grow larger than a fish that eats less. The size of a tree depends partly on how much water and sunlight it gets and how good the soil is.

Some traits are not inherited. Bulging muscles are not inherited. They come from exercise. Being able to type by touch is not inherited. This is a skill that comes through practice.

The heredity of every living thing includes instructions for keeping its body working. Heredity controls almost everything simple living things, such as worms and insects, do. In complex living things, like humans, heredity is very important, but learning is very important, too. Heredity controls how the human body works. It tells the heart how to beat and the lungs how to breathe. The brain and the ability to learn are also inherited. But what humans do with their brain and their ability to learn is not controlled by heredity.

See also **genetics; animal breeding;** and **plant breeding.**